CRITICAL APPRAISALS SERIES
General Editor: John Fletcher

A DOUBLE EXILE

African and West Indian Writing Between Two Cultures

GARETH GRIFFITHS

MARION BOYARS · LONDON

A MARION BOYARS BOOK
Distributed by
Calder & Boyars Ltd
18 Brewer Street, London W1R 4AS

First published in Great Britain in 1978 by Marion Boyars Publishers Ltd
18 Brewer Street, London W1R 4AS

©Gareth Griffiths 1978

ALL RIGHTS RESERVED

ISBN 0 7145 2622 3 (cased edition)
ISBN 0 7145 2623 1 (paperback edition)

Any paperback edition of this book whether published simultaneously with, or subsequent to, the cased edition is sold subject to the condition that it shall not, by way of trade, be lent, resold, hired out, or otherwise disposed of, without the publishers' consent, in any form of binding or cover other than that in which it is published.

No part of this publication may be reproduced, stored in a retrieval system, or transmitted, in any form or by any means, electronic, mechanical, photocopying, recording or otherwise, except brief extracts for the purposes of review, without the prior written permission of the copyright owner and publisher.

CONTENTS

ACKNOWLEDGEMENTS
7

INTRODUCTION
9

1   CELEBRATING THE PAST: FACING THE FUTURE
11

2   CONFLICTS AND CONTINUITIES:
The African Writer and his Community
49

3   CHILDHOOD AND LEAVETAKING:
Growing Up in the Caribbean
79

4   A SENSE OF PLACE
Coming to Terms with the Caribbean
110

5   MYTH AND REALITY
The Search for a Form
140

BIBLIOGRAPHY
194

INDEX
203

ACKNOWLEDGEMENTS

I wish to acknowledge the kind permission of the following to reproduce extracts from copyright material in their possession.

To William Heinemann (Educational) Pty. Ltd. for Chinua Achebe's *Things Fall Apart, Arrow of God, No Longer at Ease, A Man of the People*; for *African Writers Talking* ed. Deurden and Pieterse; for Ngugi Wa Thiong'o's *Weep not Child, The River Between, A Grain of Wheat, Homecoming*; for Elechi Amadi's *The Great Ponds;* for Christopher Okigbo's *Labyrinths*; for Michael Anthony's *Cricket in the Road, The Year in San Fernando*; for V.S. Reid's *New Day*; for Kofi Awoonor's *This Earth My Brother*.

To Penguin Books Ltd. for extracts from *Modern Poetry from Africa* ed. Moore and Beier; for V.S. Naipaul's *A House for Mr. Biswas, The Middle Passage*.

To "New Letters", University of Missouri for quotations from their special issue on African and West Indian Writing, Vol 40, No 1, Autumn, 1973.

To Houghton and Mifflin for Ayi Kwei Armah's *Fragments*.

To Jonathan Cape for *The Three Novels of Roger Mais* with an introduction by N.W. Manley.

To Oxford University Press for Gerald Moore's *Seven African Writers*, Wole Soyinka's *The Road*, William Walsh's *Commonwealth Literature*, Louis James's *The Islands in Between*.

To Longmans & Co. for Gerald Moore's *The Chosen Tongue*; for George Lamming's *In the Castle of my Skin*.

To New Beacon Books for Wilson Harris' *Tradition, the Writer and Society*.

To Faber and Faber for Wilson Harris' *Palace of the Peacock, Ascent to Omai, Black Marsden*.

To Hutchinson & Co. for Andrew Salkey's *The Late Emancipation of Jerry Stoker*.

To George Lamming for *The Emigrants, Of Age and Innocence*.

To Wingate & Co. for Samuel Selvon's *The Lonely Londoners*.

To Macgibbon & Kee for Samuel Selvon's *The Plains of Caroni*.

To Methuen & Co. for Wole Soyinka's *Madmen and Specialists*.

To the Institute for Comparative and Foreign Area Studies at the University of Washington, Seattle for excerpts from *In Person: Achebe, Awoonor & Soyinka* ed. K.L. Morell.

To Doubleday & Co. for Ayi Kwei Armah's *Why Are We So Blest?*

To Aarhus University Press for extracts from *Common Wealth* ed. Anna Rutherford.

To Evans Bros for extracts from *Caribbean Essays* ed. Andrew Salkey.

INTRODUCTION

Whatever their origin all the writers dealt with in this book share a common condition which I have called a double exile. Brought up in a culture radically different from that of England they have nevertheless chosen to write in English. They are therefore exiled culturally from the sources and traditions of that language and linguistically from the landscapes and peoples they write about.

Exile, in this sense, has often proved to be a stimulant rather than a disability to writers in this century; witness the work of Conrad, of Beckett and Ionesco for example. This has been particularly so where the distance imposed by linguistic and cultural exile has led a writer to a detachment from his time and place which has not destroyed his commitment to its special values. Fortunately this has often been the case with African and West Indian writers using English; and the proof of this lies in the range and force of their writing over the last thirty years or so.

Perhaps the single most exciting fact about this writing is that its unique qualities have often grown directly out of the problems the writers have had to face. For example, the need to record new languages or dialects in English have provided a challenge to extend the possibilities of the English language itself; whilst the urge to incorporate different social and aesthetic aims into existing English language genres has led to the development of new and distinctive forms.

Since the experiences of African and West Indian writers

using English have been different this book deals with a double exile in a simpler sense too; that is, it deals with the literature of two peoples, sharing a common experience in having been colonized and exposed to systems of racial and cultural discrimination, but quite distinct in flavour and character. I have not attempted to suggest more complicated relations between the two than this. The purpose of the book is to introduce the reader to some of the principal figures of this new writing, and some of the main directions it has taken so far. The account cannot hope to be exhaustive, nor above all, to suggest the range and variety of the work that has been done.

Through the medium of an international language these writers have not only freed the world from a heavy weight of colonial misconception, they have also defined their own place and celebrated the experience which sustains it. They have altered the image of their countries not only in the eyes of the world, but in the eyes of Africans and West Indians themselves.

CELEBRATING THE PAST: FACING THE FUTURE

The study of African writing in English has been beset by difficulties of definition. Even restricting the canon to works produced by natives of the continent begs many questions. Africans were writing in English as early as the eighteenth century, for example, Olaudah Equiano's famous account of his travels. During the nineteenth century many works were produced, though these were mainly historical, legal, and anthropological studies rather than fictional accounts. In the first three or four decades of the twentieth century the first novels, poems and plays in English begin to appear, though they are still only tentative compared with the wealth of material produced by Africans writing in French during the same period. But leaving these early attempts aside, and concentrating on the upsurge of material after the war, we can fix on the early fifties as the time when African writers in English began to establish themselves as a significant force in world literature in English. To begin with their impact was made abroad, and not at home. Almost a decade was to pass before the growing educational demand for African-English writing created a home market for the new writers. The publication of Amos Tutuola's *The Palm-Wine Drinkard* by Faber in 1952 is often cited as the moment of breakthrough. But although Tutuola's work pioneered African writing in

English abroad, it did not lead to an immediate upsurge of further writing. As Gerald Moore has said, 'Tutuola's books are far more like a fascinating cul-de-sac than the beginning of anything directly useful to other writers. The cul-de-sac is full of wonders but is nevertheless a dead-end'.[1]

Moore, writing in the early sixties, was able to see in a way that the enthusiastic early reviewers of Tutuola were not, that his work was not likely to be typical of the new writing, and that this was the result not only of the peculiar talent of Tutuola but of the difference in education and life-style between him and the majority of the new African writers who had emerged in the years between. Tutuola, educated only to High-School standard, old enough to be steeped in a natural way in the traditional culture, and without experience of contrasting cultures and societies was atypical. The new writer who succeeded him and who exploited his breakthrough into overseas publication was typically a university graduate, a 'been-to' who had travelled overseas, and a member of the relatively well-off post-Independence élite employed by the government service. The resulting differences were both formal and conceptual. Whereas Tutuola had largely adapted the loose, episodic and non-sequential structure of the traditional tale to a novel format, and had taken over much of the oral legendary and mythological material unaltered, the writers succeeding him were conscious of working in the novel *form* or the play *form*, and their adaptations were *away from* rather than *towards* this as the norm. In addition, their material was more consciously directed towards an end often defined as much by social and national aspirations as by literary purpose. The writers of the fifties and early sixties are characterized not so much by a unified style, though imitation produces strong similarities between one writer and another, as by a common purpose beyond literary aims from which only an occasional writer dissents. This purpose has perhaps best been summed up by the Nigerian novelist Chinua Achebe. Achebe has said that in his first novel *Things Fall Apart* he wanted to show

... that African peoples did not hear of culture for the first time from Europeans; that their societies were not mindless but frequently had a philosophy of great depth and value and beauty, that they had poetry and, above all, they had dignity.

(Nigeria Magazine, June 1964)

Things Fall Apart succeeds wonderfully in communicating just this, and from its publication we can date European awareness that the new literature from Africa will be the record and product of an old and deeply articulate culture too long silenced by European cultural projection during the colonial period. From this point too we can date the creation of a general impulse to record the realities of tribal life lost behind the innumerable accounts of African 'primitive customs'. Young African writers took up the challenge, and Achebe's novel was followed by a spate of imitations. For this reason many critics have felt that the publication of Achebe's novel in 1958 represents the real point at which African writing in English became a force which could not be ignored in the world at large. Since Achebe's novel is significant not only in itself but as a pattern for many which followed, we ought, perhaps, to examine it in some small detail.

The novel tells of the life of an Ibo community in what, at the time of writing, was the Eastern region of Nigeria, immediately before the arrival of white missionaries and government officials in that part of Africa. The village, or rather villages, of Umuofia, have heard rumours that white men exist but when the novel opens they are still living in a world whose problems are internal. The central figure, Okonkwo, is a man of fierce pride and masculine assertiveness, ambitious and powerful, whose drive is at least in part derived from a desire to live down a weak and socially despised father.

> With a father like Unoka, Okonkwo did not have the start in life which many young men had. He neither inherited a barn nor a title, nor even a young wife. But

in spite of these disadvantages, he had begun even in his father's lifetime to lay the foundations of a prosperous future. It was slow and painful. But he threw himself into it like one possessed. And indeed he was possessed by the fear of his father's shameful life and contemptible death.[2]

But, from the beginning of the novel, we are aware that Achebe's purpose is not to tell a story of dynastic psychology. A subtle play of suggestion is a continual feature of the simple but varied authorial comment, and this subtlety extends to the presentation of all the characters, none of whom is permitted to be just a narrative device. Thus Unoka is weak and a failure, but certain traits hint at the qualities which Okonkwo will suppress in himself which may be as equally needful to full manhood as virility and strength of purpose.

> Unoka was never happy when it came to wars. He was in fact a coward and could not bear the sight of blood. And so he changed the subject and talked about music, and his face beamed. He could hear in his mind's ear the blood-stirring and intricate rhythms of the *ekwe* and the *udu* and the *ogene*, and he could hear his own flute weaving in and out of them, decorating them with a colorful and plaintive tune. The total effect was gay and brisk, but if one picked out the flute as it went up and down and then broke up into short snatches, one saw that there was sorrow and grief there. (p. 6)

As Okonkwo's story unfolds it becomes clear that the insight and sensitivity revealed in Unoka's musical appreciation have been suppressed by his son to his cost. Okonkwo cannot afford in his eyes to show feelings which others may interpret as unmanly and weak. Thus, even in his own family, he must play the man, sometimes to the loss of his own understanding of the true situation, and to his own cost in isolation from his kith and kin.

> Okonkwo ruled his household with a heavy hand. His wives, especially the youngest, lived in perpetual fear of his fiery temper, and so did his little children. Perhaps down in his heart Okonkwo was not a cruel man. But his whole life was dominated by fear, the fear of failure and of weakness. It was deeper and more intimate than the fear of evil and capricious gods and of magic, the fear of the forest, and of the forces of nature, malevolent, red in tooth and claw. Okonkwo's fear was greater than these. It was not external but lay deep within himself. It was the fear of himself, lest he should be found to resemble his father. (p. 12-13)

With great subtlety Achebe hints that Okonkwo's aggressive masculinity is a falsification of true power since human strength has both a male and a female face, faces which meet in all fully integrated human beings. But to Okonkwo this truth is unacceptable.

> ... even now he still remembered how he had suffered when a playmate had told him that his father was *agbala*. That was how Okonkwo first came to know that *agbala* was not only another name for a woman, it could also mean a man who had taken no title. (p. 13)

But Okonkwo's stand is exposed as inadequate when at the beginning of the next chapter we are told that the Oracle of the Caves and Hills, the chief source of divination for all Umuofia is a female cult ministered by a priestess and that the Oracle is called *Agbala*.

This device illustrates how Achebe presents his world. There is no attempt in the novel to provide an explanatory gloss for non-Ibo readers. We learn the significance and meaning of the terms and customs we encounter through the action itself, and thus our engagement with the world of Umuofia, is a complete and absorbing one.

The tension of Okonkwo comes to a head with the death of Ikemefuna, a young boy who has been given to Umuofia in reparation for the death of an Umuofia woman in the neighbouring village of Mbaino. Okonkwo, who has been asked to look after the boy by Umuofia, has come to stand as surrogate father to Ikemefuna who has formed deep attachments in his family, especially with Okonkwo's son Nwoye, who the old man fears shows the weakness and womanliness of his grandfather. After a number of years the Oracle announces that Ikemefuna must die, and against the advice of the old man, Ezeudu, Okonkwo takes part in the killing, actually striking the boy down with his matchet. From this point the decline in Okonkwo's fortune begins, and the estrangement from his son Nwoye deepens.

Okonkwo's offence is not that he has done wrong, since Ikemefuna's death was necessary and just; but that he has done more than he was strictly called upon to perform. As his friend Obierika tells him, he need not have done the deed, though he could not dispute it. But the cause of his excess is, of course, his fear not his zeal.

> He heard Ikemefuna cry, 'My father they have killed me,' as he ran towards him. Dazed with fear, Okonkwo drew his machete and cut him down. He was afraid of being thought weak. (p. 55)

This is the central and pervasive irony of Okonkwo's tragedy, that he is destroyed not because of his flaws but because he performs more than is expected of him. He sacrifices his personal life to an exaggerated and even pathological sense of communal duty. Though in a society like Umuofia, where the law is literally in the mouths of the old, to ignore the warning of Ezeudu is to act in defiance of the values of his society. Things have already begun to fall apart when that which is necessary and just ceases to be tempered by moderation and flexibility.

This irony is deepened and extended by Achebe's presentation of Nwoye. After Ikemefuna's death the latent resentment of Nwoye against his father, and against the cruelty of his world urges him towards the new force in Umuofia represented by the struggling, newly-introduced mission-church. In an almost complete reversal of Okonkwo's stand, Nwoye puts personal feeling above social responsibility. His capacity for personal relationships, and the finer sensibility which results is a kind of advance, but at the cost of a loss of pride, of social unity and clarity of purpose. There is no simple judgement involved here. Nwoye's viewpoint is not presented as better or worse than Okonkwo's. As Achebe himself has written, each man must dance the dance of his times.

Okonkwo's assertiveness leads to disaster when he accidentally kills a fellow clansman. He must wipe out the offence by a seven year exile with his mother's clan. At the end of the novel, Okonkwo returns to Umuofia to find that the forces which threaten it have all but completed their work. The white man, who at his departure had been a distant if potent threat has now all but completed his invasion. The mission church which, under its first pastor Mr. Brown, had been mindful if opposed to traditional custom is now, under the Reverend Smith, openly destructive. During his exile Okonkwo has dreamed of returning to Umuofia and reasserting his claim to be a leader of his clan. But he quickly realizes that Umuofia has lost heart and makes a desperate attempt to get his fellow clansmen to recognize the need to fight for their survival.

> The clan had undergone such profound change during his exile that it was barely recognizable. The new religion and government and the trading stores were very much in the people's eyes and minds. There were still many who saw these new institutions as evil, but even they talked and thought about little else ...
>
> Okonkwo was deeply grieved. And it was not just a personal grief. He mourned for the clan, which he saw breaking up and falling apart, and he mourned for the warlike men of Umuofia who had so unaccountably become soft like women. (p. 165)

Finally persuading his fellow elders that action must be taken, Okonkwo leads the masked spirits of the clan to the mission which they burn down. For a brief while he feels a return of hope but this is quickly dashed when he is arrested and thrown into prison. Returning to Umuofia he makes one last effort to persuade his fellow clansmen that they must fight or be overthrown. For the last time he gathers the clan but the meeting in the village *ilo* is interrupted by the arrival of the court messengers with orders from the District Commissioner that the meeting is to stop. Provoked beyond endurance by this last insult Okonkwo cuts one of the messengers down. But in that same moment he learns that the erosion is too far advanced and he is alone.

> Okonkwo stood looking at the dead man. He knew that Umuofia would not go to war. He knew because they had let the other messengers escape. They had broken into tumult. He discerned fright in that tumult. (p. 184)

Okonkwo's suicide which follows is reported in a way which takes us to the heart of Achebe's method and demonstrates the skill and subtlety of his writing. In the final chapter the white District Commissioner arrives at the village. He is intent on obtaining retribution, but Okonkwo's suicide has forestalled him. Two separate views of what follows are then interwoven, that of the D.C. and that of Obierika, Okonkwo's friend and clansman. The commissioner is fascinated by the refusal of the 'tribe' to handle the dead body, since Okonkwo's suicide has rendered him untouchable. He, we are told, is a 'student of primitive customs'. The phrase immediately transfers us from the inner view sustained throughout the novel to an alternative outer view of all we have been shown. We suddenly become aware that what we have been reading is an English which has reproduced through its rhythm, syntax and structure as well as its proverbial patterning and social commentary, Ibo thoughts and speech patterns. Now we are forced suddenly to see ourselves as we have been in the act of reading, outsiders looking in.

Obierika, who had been gazing steadily at his friend's dangling body, turned suddenly to the District Commissioner, and said ferociously: 'That man was one of the greatest men in Umuofia. You drove him to kill himself; and now he will be buried like a dog ...' He could not say more. His voice trembled and choked his words. 'Shut up!' shouted one of the messengers, quite unnecessarily. (p. 187)

Unnecessarily because not only is Obierika overcome, but in any case the D.C. could not understand a word he said, speaking as he does in the 'savage' speech of Umuofia. And we become terribly aware that, prior to reading this novel, we would be standing in the white commissioner's shoes, outsiders looking in and seeing nothing. To the commissioner the passionate and terrible events Achebe has chronicled excite only the idea that he may make use of this 'episode' to write a whole, or at least a part, chapter of his book *The Pacification of the Primitive Tribes of the Lower Niger*.

It is in this attempt to go 'inside' the experience of the past that *Things Fall Apart* caught the imagination of a whole generation of African writers. But, of course, there was a danger in this as in any approach, a danger which Achebe's skill and breadth of vision avoids, but which became a trap for many of the poorer imitators of his fiction. Nowhere in his treatment of the past does Achebe suggest that a tribal society was a simple, idyllic one, nor does he shy away from the degree of complicity which it bears in its own destruction. As a result his portrait is all the more powerful, and his implied indictment of colonialism and its falsifications of the past all the more credible and forceful. In this respect, the new African writers using English seemed to be reacting against the anthropological romanticism of their earlier precursors using French. The philosophy of négritude, so important in African-French writing has never taken root in African-writing in English. Wole Soyinka's comment that the tiger has no need to proclaim its tigritude is an expression of a general attitude which Achebe seems to share. But not all the younger writers, fired by a desire to do for their own cultural past what Achebe had done for that of the Ibo could manage the same realism and clarity of vision. It is of these, perhaps, that Soyinka was thinking when in 1968, in an article published while he was still in a Federal jail, he warned that,

> We (Africans) whose humanity the poets celebrated before the proof, whose lyric innocence was daily questioned by the pages of the newspapers, are now being forced by disaster, not foresight, to a reconsideration of our relationship with the outer world ... The myth of irrational nobility, of a racial essence that must come to the rescue of the white depravity, has run its full course. It never in fact existed, for this was not the problem but the camouflage.[3]

For Achebe, as for Soyinka in plays like *A Dance of the Forest*, *The Lion and the Jewel* etc., the celebration of the past and of traditional values and practices is an attempt to recover a full human experience and not to create a false paradisal perfection. This clear-eyed act of celebration is even more central to Achebe's third novel *Arrow of God* which again deals with the colonial onslaught and its destructive effect on traditional tribal life.

Arrow of God[4] is Achebe's longest and most complex novel to date. The story centres on Ezeulu, the priest of Ulu, chief deity of the villages of Umuaro. Ezeulu is a proud and independent man whose human loyalty to his people is tempered by his awareness that, as Ulu's priest, he has also a divine loyalty which makes him an 'arrow in the bow of his god'. To many of his neighbours and rivals his fierce and uncompromising struggle to reconcile these demands and remain true to both people and Gods is a sign of his personal pride and ambition. The fiercely democratic Ibo social system must, innately, struggle to limit aspiration of this kind; and the clash between Ezeulu and his society is a normal one, part of the system of checks and balances by which Ibo tribal life regulates the exercise of power by the strong over the weak. It is Ezeulu's tragedy that a new factor is introduced into the system by the presence of the white man. Ezeulu's truthfulness has forced him to witness against his own people in a land-dispute heard before the white District Commissioner. This act serves to crystallize the opposition against him within the tribe. It also causes the D.C., aptly named Winterbottom, to decide to make Ezeulu the 'chief' of Umuaro under the new system of Indirect Rule by native chiefs which the government requires the Ibo to adopt, though such a system is quite alien to the fundamentally democratic character of Ibo society. When Ezeulu refuses this privilege he is cast into prison where he remains for several months. Since his absence makes him unable to perform his function as priest and consume the requisite number of ceremonial yams by which the vital Feast of the New Yams is calculated, this provokes a head-on clash between Ezeulu and his opponents within the tribe. He refuses to confirm the feast, thus condemning the village to hardship and hunger. In so doing he argues that he is only 'an arrow in the bow of his god'; and we are witness to Ulu's command that he should not yield. But to his opponents his attitude is the result of a pride which puts his dignity before the welfare of his people; and, indeed, it is clear that Ezeulu is, at least in part, motivated by a desire for revenge, and sees in his situation a tool designed by Ulu with which he can chastise his opponents.

The subtlety with which Achebe shows the interaction of the conflict within the tribe and the larger conflict between traditional tribal life and the new forces of white colonialism is a primary feature of the novel's success. Many incidents, images and sub-plots are woven through the main narrative, but all skilfully direct us to a deeper understanding of Ezeulu's complex character and the difficulties of the situation in which he finds himself. A primary irony is the fact that Ezeulu himself is not properly aware of the power of the forces he invokes by his decision; and this limitation of insight is paralleled by that of Winterbottom, who has no real understanding of the effects of his actions within the world he rules. Both seek to make use of part of a world from which they are excluded and of which they know next to nothing. In each case Achebe, from his unique perspective, that 'double exile' I have discussed in the introduction, presents us with a picture of the strange unity of prejudice, perceptions, loyalties and demands which go to make up a culture. When two such unities meet head-on they inevitably grind down all those rash enough to stand in their way, for as Kenneth Post has remarked 'two totalities cannot co-exist and both remain intact'.[5]

But this awareness of the cultural consequences of the book's action is never allowed to dominate the foreground. We are not dealing with an historical thesis masquerading as a novel. Achebe's historical perception is totally conveyed through the personal tragedy of Ezeulu, and the actual events of Umuaro's time and place. It is this concrete quality which gives the story its bite and effect. As William Walsh has said,

> Chinua Achebe's is the natural imagination of the novelist which works through particular events and personalities and discriminated shades of being and feeling. It is not surprising, therefore, that the general event is involved in the particular, and that the reader takes, without any feeling that he or the structure of the novel is being manipulated, the sense in which the collapse of the whole society is implied in the priest's fall.[6]

Most critical accounts of the novel centre too exclusively on the dilemma of Ezeulu in a personal and psychological way. They question whether or not Ezeulu is motivated by his personal desire to punish the people of Umuaro for not listening to his advice, or is indeed an arrow in the bow of his god. Echoing the novel's own statement of the issue they speculate whether

'A priest like Ezeulu leads a god to ruin himself. It has happened before.'

'Or perhaps a god like Ulu leads a priest to ruin himself.' (p. 266)

Although the psychological character of Ezeulu is important, and Achebe does indeed provide us with a rich portrait of a complex figure, belying comments that African novels 'lack characterization', there is a further level to which attention has been too infrequently drawn. The viewpoint has been best expressed by the Ghanaian writer Kofi Awoonor, who says

> Chinua Achebe's *Arrow of God* is one of the most eloquent statements on the restorative role of the artist, who is at times – and most times – equivalent to the priest in the community. He goes before the people, accepts in his priestly role the pain and ecstasy of his burden, and to borrow a phrase from Achebe, accepts all the beatings like the trembling ram on the road to the sacrifice. One of the most central passages in *Arrow of God*, to which western critics hardly pay any attention, is the incredible scene of Ezeulu's re-enactment of the mythic drama of the founding of Ulu. This passage is unsurpassed in dramatic intensity, poetic evocation, and the restatement of the total *human* condition. Ezeulu is the best amalgam of the duality of god and man, combining both the intellectual grasp of the observable and the intuitive understanding of the divine. The arcane and the mysterious can join with the mundane. The contradictions are endemic and expectable. So he, who stood for the principle of the mask-watchers not standing in one place, was bypassed when his hesitation and ultimate refusal to eat the sacred yam threatened the very survival of the whole community. Umuaro chose life, in the face of inexplicable death, and their choice, contrary to what most critics will have us believe, is not a victory for the Christian faith, but a restatement of the very basic ontological principle of survival.

The perspective which this opens allows us to see the proper role of the communal world in the action of the novel, and to avoid a false distinction of character and story line from description of traditional Ibo life. In this novel the characters grow out of the world described, and the events are part of their interaction.

Thus when Ezeulu is confronted by the Mask at the end of chapter eighteen we are not being shown merely an interesting piece of local colour but a key to the relationships between Ezeulu, his role and his community which goes directly to the heart of the decision with which the next chapter opens, the decision to withhold the announcement of the feast of the New Yam.

> Meanwhile the Mask had proceeded to the *okwolo* to salute some of the elders.
> 'Ezeulu de-de-de-de-dei,' it said.
> 'Our father, my hand is on the ground,' replied the Chief Priest.
> 'Ezeulu, do you know me?'
> 'How can a man know you who are beyond human knowledge?'
> 'Ezeulu, our Mask salutes you,' it sang. (p. 250)

The fact that this exchange is formalized, and that the words of the priest and the Mask are ritualized and traditional, bound in a continuity of question and response, reinforces rather than undermines its function in the novel. The passage makes clear the seriousness and awesomeness of Ezeulu's decision to abrogate a godlike power to which he is only partly heir. Ezeulu in this brief exchange with the Mask asserts his continuity with all mortal men, with whom he shares the obligations of ritual as he does the frailties of flesh. Thus his decision to ignore this duality within himself is presented in and through our awareness of the whole community of actions by which he is bound, that of his village, of his time, and of his universe.

At the end Ezeulu's mortality is brought home to us with a gravity and a dignity which lends a majesty to his defeat. With the death of his son Obika Ezeulu's faith in the continuity of his will and Ulu's is broken.

> ... The matchet fell from his hand and he slumped down on both knees besides the body. 'My son,' he cried, 'Ulu, were you there when this happened to me?' He hid his face on Obika's chest. (p. 284-285)

In this novel, as in *Things Fall Apart*, the proverbial commentary which is so central a feature of the Ibo language is used as a device to point the meaning of episode and character. Now, with the collapse of Ezeulu's mind the proverbial code seems to lose its power as the priest's grief-stricken conscience races over its paths, seeking an assurance which the old wisdom can no longer yield.

> ... Why, he asked himself, again and again, why had Ulu chosen to deal thus with him, to strike him down and cover him with mud? What was his offence? Had he not divined the god's will and obeyed it? When was it ever heard that a child was scalded by the piece of yam its own mother put in its palm? What man would send his son with a potsherd to bring fire from a neighbour's hut and then unleash rain on him? Who ever sent his son up the palm to gather nuts and then took an axe and felled the tree? But today such a thing had happened before the eyes of all. What could it point to but the collapse and ruin of all things? (p. 286)

Though the end of the novel has sometimes been read as a simple assertion that Ezeulu's actions have unwittingly called into being a new support for the intruding Christian missionaries the actual text offers no such firm conclusion. The authorial comment remains tentative and speculative. It offers the conclusions as they occur, dramatically rendered in the voices of those who proffer them. The belief of the elders of Umuaro that '... the issue was simple. Their god had taken sides with them against their headstrong and ambitious priest ...' (p. 287); or the reported effect of Ezeulu's stand on the loyalties of the people '... Thereafter any yam that was harvested in the man's fields was harvested in the name of the son ...' (p. 287) should not be mistaken for direct authorial comment. The results of the actions of men are as unsure a guide to the truth as are their intentions. What remains is a picture of the human struggle with an often incomprehensible reality, whose causes and effects seem often equally the creations and creators of those who must, perforce, endure them.

To fully understand Achebe's achievement and its importance as an example to others it is important to define the general problem which, as an African writer, he faced. This problem was to record in English the internal pulse of a culture in which English was almost completely unknown. Since this is a problem faced by many of the writers in this book it is worth outlining how Achebe has succeeded in converting this difficulty into a new tool for insight and communication.

There is an Ibo saying, which Achebe has frequently quoted, to the effect that 'proverbs are the palm oil with which words are eaten.' This emphasises that the Ibo culture prior to colonization was an oral culture, and one, therefore, in which traditional wisdom and experience were encapsulated and handed down from generation to generation in proverbial sayings, stories and myths. Thus, for the Ibo the central linguistic art is the art of oratory and conversation. I have already said in outlining the action of *Things Fall Apart* that in such a society law is in the mouths of the old. An old man like Ezeudu is the library of the society, and proverbs and stories are its books. But, of course, Achebe is aware that as a modern Ibo writer he is not the recipient of such an unadulterated tradition. By his education and by his decision to write in English which followed from it, he is unable to make a direct and unchanged use of the traditional Ibo

CELEBRATING THE PAST

structures. In the case of *Things Fall Apart*, therefore, dealing as it does with a society still self-sufficient and unadulterated, his task is to discover an English idiom which will accomodate the new material and indicate its original form in the new language. This he does by a syntax which lends itself to a slow, climactic piling of unit upon unit; simple but strong phrasing, relying heavily for structural unity on repetition of phrase and image; a skilled use of the Ibo repertory of proverbs, not as 'local colour' but as part of the narrative texture and a tool of the author's rhetorical control; and, above all, a refusal to explain and gloss where the narrative itself provides the information for an attentive and engaged reader. The overall result, as I have said, is that the reader is involved with the world of Umuofia in an inner way which becomes in itself part of the book's essential 'meaning'. The oral element is retained in the very structure by which each unit is defined clearly in its time and place.

> The feast of the New Yam was approaching ...
> For the first time in three nights ...
> The last big rains of the year were falling ...
> When nearly two years later ...

And many other similar chapter and paragraph openings. While at moments one is reminded of the rhythms and tone of the tale and story that is the book in Umuofia, e.g. 'There was a wealthy man in Okonkwo's village who had three barns ...' Yet none of this implies any lack of sophistication or anything but the most complete control of the material to shape a story of great subtlety. Critics who have commented on the simplicity of Achebe's style have sometimes confused it with naivety, but it is only the units of the narrative that are simple, not their accumulated interaction in the structure. Because the structure is based on interrelated and repeated units of sense Achebe can retain a direct link with the tone and pattern of oral narrative and so illustrate the culture as he celebrates its passing.

The impetus which *Things Fall Apart* (1958) and *Arrow of*

God (1964) gave to African writers to re-discover their own version of their past was quickly taken up. A list of African novels in English influenced by Achebe would be a long one. Often, of course, the influence was a disastrous one, with young writers adopting the form without the substance of his achievement. Too often the resulting novels are merely thinly-disguised sociological and historical reconstructions, valuable in this respect, but hardly of interest as works of art. Benjamin Akiga, Ntieyong Udo Akpan, T.M. Aluko and Onuora Nzekwu are just a few of the Nigerian novelists whose work shows the influence of Achebe without his attention to form and language. Even the best of these, Nzekwu for example, seem top-heavy with detail of custom and tradition. Describing Nzekwu's work Gerald Moore has said,

> (He) has not yet grasped that the retailing of anthropological matter for its own sake is mere exoticism in a work of creative art. It can be used only as Achebe uses it, to make the life before us more actual, to surround it with its own dignity, beauty or cruelty in its own moment of time and place.[8]

This comment may stand as epitaph to all those writers who have found Achebe difficult to follow. But not all the writers whose work shows Achebe's influence have been swamped by his example. Some have realized that his importance as a guide lay not only in his stated purpose, to celebrate the past, but also in the originality and appropriateness of the forms he developed to do this. And they have been aware that in their own treatment a simple imitation of purpose divorced from the development of a personal style and an individual viewpoint is not enough.

Elechi Amadi is a Nigerian writer who has succeeded in making an original and unusual personal vision from the history of his people. In his two published novels, *The Concubine* (1966) and *The Great Ponds* (1969) we are taken into a society undisturbed by outside forces, a self-contained society in which traditional practices have not yet been challenged by the outside world. Only the end of *The Great Ponds*, with its reference to the international flu-epidemic of 1918 allows us to place the action in a world context. For the rest we are drawn into the life of a community whose values are intact and whose drama is self-generated. The late date of the main reference in *The Great Ponds* to European influences serves to remind us of the longevity of the survival of an independent tribal life, and to remind us too of how short a time in comparison is occupied by the contemporary African experience of colonization and national independence. In a very perceptive lecture Alistair Niven has drawn our attention to the importance of recognizing that the world depicted by Amadi is one close to contemporary experience, arguably even still a living part of it.

> To treat *The Concubine*, in particular, but *The Great Ponds* too, merely as historical reconstructions of a vanished era is to miss the relevance of their moral statement to the Africa of today, an Africa that for the massive majority outside the largest towns is not enormously different from that which Amadi here describes.[9]

Thus, for Niven, Amadi's purpose is subtly different to Achebe's, not only to recreate and celebrate the past, but through the past to restate to his contemporaries the durability of its traditions and values. For Niven,

> Amadi, perhaps more truly than any other West African writer including Achebe, has expressed the enduring values of African culture, and whereas Achebe seems pessimistic about whether these values have the strength to survive, Amadi implies that they have not only the strength but the credibility.[10]

Both Amadi's novels centre, as Niven points out, on the 'portrayal of man's relations to the gods'[11]. In *The Concubine* we trace the misfortunes of the beautiful but fey Ihuoma, who brings destruction to all the men who love her. Towards the end of the novel we learn that the root cause is that she is the mortal reincarnation of a wife of the sea-god, whose jealousy of her earthly lovers encompasses their destruction. Similarly, in *The Great Ponds*, the story of the struggle between two rival villages in a clan for the possession of a rich fishing pond resolves itself into the story of one man's struggle to survive an encounter with the divine when he takes an oath binding himself to destruction to back up his village's claim to the truth. The novel resolves itself when a flu epidemic sweeps down on the village. Puzzled by the totally unknown ailment which they call Wonjo, the villagers see it as the work of the god Ogbunabali, to whom Olumba's oath was made. When they discover that their rival village, and, indeed, the world beyond the clan is also infected, their puzzlement deepens. What can the visitation mean? In the face of the onslaught of disease the traditional practices crumble, and the power of the clan and its dibias (priests) are unable to prevail against it. With the disappearance of the remedies of the past and the break-up of morale in the face of overwhelming numbers of deaths the fate which has overcome the village can only be seen in apocalyptic terms. The only reality within the communal imagination large enough to encompass this new experience is the growing conviction that Wonjo is the instrument of the final dissolution.

> Olumba was a sight as he beat the *ikoro*. With his sunken eyes and wild beard he looked like a risen skeleton beating the ikoro for the last time to announce the end of the world.[12]

In the face of this threat the issues of the recent war over the pond ceases to have significance. The defeat of the village's claim, not through Olumba's death under the oath, but through the madness of their most implacable opponent's suicide in its water, which renders the pond unusable, serves only to underline the greater defeat of Wonjo. Wonjo itself, no doubt, takes on for a modern reader a symbolic force, and comes to represent the outside world which will break up the tribal life. The last line of the novel, with its shift to an outside stance, underlines this

> But it was only the beginning. Wonjo, as the villagers called the Great Influenza of 1918, was to claim a grand total of some twenty million lives all over the world.
> (*The Great Ponds* p. 217)

Yet, within the overall structure of the story this final twist seems almost gratuitous. The tragedy of Wonjo is part of the unceasing struggle to understand the world the people of Amokachi inhabit and to adapt code and tradition to master it. That the code and traditions fail is less a denial of them than an expression of their limitations, limitations they share with all human systems. Just as Ekwueme's death at the end of *The Concubine* asserts man's powerlessness when faced by the gods, so Wonjo and its effect asserts the truth that man will always be subject to forces beyond his understanding, forces which in African terms find expression in the dense pattern of traditional myth and ritual. As Alistair Niven has stated, Amadi's novels argue for the integrity of African myth.

> He is not suggesting that the traditional beliefs of his people are actually true. He does suggest, however, that they supply for a village like Amokachi a source of spiritual value.[13]

Niven's spirited defence of Amadi may draw attention to the work of one of the more interesting recent African writers. Amadi's two novels both show structural weaknesses. He tends to place significant pieces of information late in the narrative which may make a reader feel too consciously manipulated; and he lacks the linguistic richness and subtlety of Achebe. But his novels serve to show how the theme of recovery and continuity may be related effectively to the continuing problems facing a contemporary reader.

More significant, perhaps, as an example of the widespread influence of Achebe's work and of the theme of celebration of the past is the work of Ngugi Wa Thiong'o (James Ngugi). Ngugi is a Kenyan, and the earliest writer from East Africa to have his work widely published abroad. His novels illustrate how, despite profound cultural and historical differences in the backgrounds of the various writers in West and East Africa, the desire to record the truth about the past and the destructive impact of colonialism on the integrity of traditional life became an almost universal impulse for writers of the first wave. Ngugi had readily acknowledged the influence of Achebe and other West African writers, and defines with great clarity the importance of their work to young writers elsewhere in Africa who were inspired by them to record their own experience and that of their peoples. He has said,

> I had read Chinua Achebe, I had read Ekwensi and I think some of the West Indian writers, and I think these people set my imagination flying ... What the African writers did for me in a way that no other English writer could do for me was to make me feel that they were really speaking to me: the situation about which they were writing was one which was immediate to me, and also I found for the first time I was talking with my own people. I was talking with characters whom I knew, in a way, who had agonies which I had seen with our own people in Kenya and at that point I felt that ... I could write as well.[14]

As his later comments have made clear[15], Ngugi was to come to see the same continuity of experience in the work of West Indians like George Lamming. This continuity is not only cultural but political, a continuity of peasant communities disrupted by and then exploited in the favour of colonial powers. Ngugi clearly sees himself not only as an African, but as a 'Third World' novelist. For him there can be no separation of the two impulses, the impulse to recover and recreate and the impulse to analyze the cause in political terms. Yet, despite this assertion, the strength of his writing lies not in polemic but in the sensitivity and skill with which he goes inside the individual experiencing the flow of historical events. All four of his novels to date reveal a temperamental bias towards the exploration of inner state rather than outward event. Ngugi's typical concern has been the inner flow of a character's thought as he reflects on the past, the present and the future and relates each event to the growth of his own personality and to the times he lives in. His admiration for the work of the West Indian George Lamming probably reflects a similar attempt in that writer to relate the individual and his feelings to the history of his times. More important, perhaps, to our immediate concern is the clear difference this bias gives to Ngugi's work compared with the West African writers, especially Achebe, who influenced him. With Achebe a character's inner reactions are usually displayed dramatically in and through his reactions to his society, and in a novel like *Things Fall Apart* we are only rarely allowed to 'go behind' Okonkwo and see directly how he is responding to events. Ngugi's first two novels, *The River Between* (written first, though not published until 1965) and *Weep Not, Child* (1964) are set in a period after the Gikuyu people have been contacted by European missionaries and settlers. The greater role the European plays in the action of both, especially in *Weep Not, Child*, reflects the East African colonial pattern, where settlement was widespread. *The River Between* is the 'contact' novel, dealing as it does with the disruptive effect of Christian missionary activity on the traditional life of the two villages on either bank of the River Honia. Waiyaki, the young protagonist, is the living result of the meeting of old and new. A product of the missionary schools, he sees the liberating possibilities in education and strives to set up schools for his people. But, at the same time, he is aware of the disruptive effect of Christianity on traditional life, and so rebels against missionary control of the education system. This movement to initiate Independent Schools is historically accurate. Waiyaki's dream is that those who remain faithful to the rites of the tribe should not thereby be deprived of the benefits of literacy. But, as we saw in the case of *Arrow of God*, two totalities may not coexist intact, and those who strive for their reconciliation are often crushed between them, as Waiyaki is. Only at the very end of the novel does he realize that 'Education for an oppressed people is not all.' He has neglected the main task, to unify the divided tribes and the traditional and Christian factions in a political unity which can withstand the onslaught of the colonizers who have followed in the missionaries' wake. He reflects that in one sense his opponents had been right.

> People wanted action now. The stirrings in the hills were an awakening to the shame and humiliation of their condition. Their isolation had been violated. But what action was needed? What had he to do now? How could he organize people into a political organization when they were so torn with strife and disunity? Now he knew what he would preach if he ever got another chance: education for unity. Unity for political freedom.[16]

Of course he is too late and the book ends with his trial.

The River Between is often praised for the force of its symbolic patterning, with river, ridge and settlements invoked in a ritual geography which underlines the divisions and meanings of the various forces at work in the society. But I must admit to finding the use of symbolism too heavy and occasionally banal,

> The land was now silent. The two ridges lay side by side, hidden in the darkness. And Honia river went on flowing between them, down through the valley of life ...
> (*The River Between*, p. 175)

The real achievement of the novel seems to me to be the capacity Ngugi shows even in this apprentice work to go inside the minds of his characters and reveal the processes of self-doubt and inner questioning through which men falter in their purpose and visions are undone. This subtlety of character portrayal is not maintained throughout, and

Waiyaki can be very wooden and unlifelike when he is forced into a Christ-like role in the novel's symbolic pattern. But it does allow for a wide range of sympathy and a presentation of all the characters as motivated by understandable responses, whether they are condemned by the action as mistaken or not.

Weep Not, Child is set later when white settlers have deprived the Gikuyu of most of their traditional land, and one of the book's primary ironies is achieved by the subtle contrast of the attitude of Howlands, the white farmer, and Ngotho, his farmhand, to the land they both work. Howland's affection for Ngotho, based on the latter's obvious concern for the land, is profoundly ironic, since he is not aware that it is his feeling for the land which is a reflection of Ngotho's instinctive feeling, and not the other way around. But the heart of the book is once again the story of the education into political awareness of Ngotho's young son, Njoroge. Again, obsessed initially with education for its own sake. Njoroge learns under the stress of the Mau-Mau emergency that 'Education was good only because it would lead to the recovery of the lost lands'[17]. This politicization of Njoroge is not just a polemic essay woven into the narrative line but is fully integrated with the exploration of his feelings and understanding as he grows to maturity under the impact of events. If the message is here sometimes overstressed and heavily managed Ngugi nevertheless again demonstrates that the core of his interest is always the formation of experience in the mind of his characters. At the heart of his technique is the urge to go inside the minds of his characters so that they live the full effect of the history of their times for themselves and the reader.

> Njorogo did not want to be like his father working for a white man, or, worse, for an Indian. Father had said that the work was hard and had asked him to escape from the same conditions. Yes, he would. He would be different, and he would help all his brothers. Before he

went to sleep he prayed, 'Lord, help me get learning. I want to help my father and mothers. And Kamau and all my other brothers. I ask you all this through Jesus Christ, our Lord, Amen.'

He remembered something else.

'... And help me god so that Mwihaki may not beat me in class. And God ...'

He fell asleep and dreamed of education in England.

(*Weep Not, Child* pp. 49-50)

Ngugi's third novel, *A Grain of Wheat*, is a triumphant vindication of his technique in a novel of genuine stature and assurance. Set in the period leading up to Kenyan Independence it gathers up the meanings of the past and reviews them in the face of the future which the political struggle has finally achieved for the Kenyan people.

A Grain of Wheat is a difficult book to describe, since its effect depends so much on the subtle correspondences invoked between time present and time past. The story begins *in medias res* and the reader is gradually allowed to become aware of the secret guilt which nearly all the characters bear as a result of their actions or inactions during the period of the Emergency. Ngugi has said that,

> ... in the Kenyan scene of the last sixty years you cannot separate economics and culture from politics. The three are interwoven. A cultural assertion was an integral part of the political and economic struggle.[18]

Thus there is a continual pattern of reference to the early days of the Independence movement, and beyond these to the period of colonization and missionary infiltration. Behind all these levels of historical time the novel continually relates its insights to the traditional events of Gikuyu culture, and ironically patterns these in counterpoint with the Biblical myths which the Gikuyu have taken over and used to supplement and reinforce their own stories of creation and conflict. These complex patternings allow even the smallest and apparently least significant passage to reverberate with implications.

> Mumbi often went to the station platforms on Sundays. The rattling train always thrilled her. At times she longed to be the train itself. But she never went to the dances in the forest. She always came back home, after the train, and with one or two other girls, would cook, or undo and re-do their hair. Her dark eyes had a dreamy look that longed for something the village could not give. She lay in the sun and ardently yearned for a life in which love and heroism, suffering and martyrdom were possible. She was young. She had fed on stories in which Gikuyu women braved the terrors of the forest to save people, of beautiful girls given to the gods as sacrifice before the rains. In the Old Testament she often saw herself as Esther: so she revelled in that moment when Esther finally answers King Asahuera's question and dramatically points at Haman, saying: The adversary and enemy is the wicked Haman. She enjoyed the admiration she excited in men's eyes. When she laughed, she threw back her head and her neck would gleam in the firelight.[19]

A passage like this is rich in implication both within itself and through allusion to further episodes in the novel. For example, in the ironic contrast between Mumbi's dreams and her fate; in the contrast we are to see between her imagined delight in the role of accuser, and the anguish she endures when she faces this experience in real life; and in the delicate allusion at the end to the mythic figure Wangu Makeri whose dancing drove men wild with desire, and whose fate was to be destroyed by those same men when she overstepped herself and danced naked before her admirers. (pp. 14-15)

The action of the novel opens in the days immediately preceding the celebrations of Kenyan Independence, 'the days of Uhuru na Kazi'. The central figure, Mugo (the name again has implications in Gikuyu culture as that of the famous tribal seer who had predicted the coming of the white man and his final expulsion from the tribal homeland) is a man haunted by guilt. As the novel unfolds we gradually learn that he is the betrayer of the freedom fighter Kihika, the brother of his neighbour Mumbi. Ironically, Mugo is considered a hero by his fellows because after his betrayal of Kihika he had heroically resisted when a soldier attempted to beat a pregnant woman building a defensive moat around the village. The surviving leaders of the freedom fighters wish Mugo to act as spokesman for the village at the Uhuru celebrations. This story of secret guilt, and ironic confusion, is the skeleton of a plot in which gradually Ngugi reveals the hidden core of guilt and disillusionment at the heart of each of the novel's main characters. Most of the villagers blame Kihika's betrayal on Karanja, a local trader whom the authorities had made chief under the emergency laws and who had assumed command of the home-guard unit in the village. Karanja has raped Mumbi, who bears him a child. Mumbi's husband Gikonyo, himself haunted by guilt because of his secret betrayal of his oath in the detention camp, is estranged from Mumbi, refusing to believe that she was not a willing accomplice in the act. Beyond these central figures each of the other characters is shown to be acting out an existence only made tolerable by the suppression of some event in the past. This is true not only of the Gikuyu characters, but of the European figures too, whose portrayal in the novel is detailed and sensitive. Thus the leader of the European anti-Mau Mau forces, John Thompson, and his wife Margery, as well as the pathetic spinsterish Dr. Lynde are all involved in a similar pattern of guilt and suppression.

Through these multiple acts of secrecy and self-deception Ngugi shows how the historical force of the struggle for freedom has marked all the participants. Nobody is free from the cost of pain and suffering involved in the birth of the new nation. The central martyr, Kihika, is perhaps most fortunate in that his betrayal and execution have rendered him immune. For those left the task is less easy. They have to discover a way to live with themselves and to bury the past and its shame and guilt. Only then will they be free to face the new problems and rewards of independence.

By the end of the novel the whole land has been choked by a spider's web of interlocking suspicion, betrayal and guilt. Each individual character and situation is significant not only in itself, but as part of a poisonous net which must be cast off if life is to renew itself. As the novel's title suggests, the husk of the old seed must rot and wither away for the new shoot to come forth.

The tensions come to a climax on the day of the Uhuru celebrations. The returned forest-fighters, led by Koinandu and General R., plan to expose Karanja as the betrayer of Kihika before the crowd assembled to celebrate the day of freedom. As the day approaches Mugo feels the burden of his secret more and more. In a similar way all the other characters are forced to review their actions. Uhuru is a day of liberation, and yet each man is trapped in his own past. There is no way in which a new flag can be raised to signify a rebirth for the individual.

The end of the celebration arrives and the moment comes when General R. must name Karanja as the betrayer of Kihika, but before he can do so Mugo comes forward and confesses to the crime. He is later tried, and presumably executed. The day of Uhuru ends in confusion and bitterness.

Uhuru with all its amplitude and hope serves as a great catalyst. It has swept away not only the bitterness and oppression of the colonial days, but also the security of the past. The old people, Warui and Wambui are as much at a loss as the young to account for the experiences which have brought them their long-coveted independence. Mugo's confession and trial seems to sum up the inner disillusion which each of the characters must struggle against.

> Wambui sat on and watched the drizzle and the grey mist for a few minutes. Darkness was creeping into the

hut. Wambui was lost in a solid consciousness of a terrible anti-climax to her activities in the fight for freedom. Perhaps we should not have tried him, she muttered. Then she shook herself, trying to bring her thoughts to the present. I must light the fire. First I must sweep the room. How dirt can so quickly collect in a clean hut! (pp. 275-76)

But she did not rise to do anything.

Nevertheless the novel ends on a note of anticipation. Gikonyo has fallen in the Uhuru day race and broken his arm. While he recuperates in the hospital he reflects on the stool he always meant to carve as a marriage gift for Mumbi. He wonders what he should represent on it: 'three grim-faced figures, sweating under a weight', the people and their past of oppression, the eternal underlying truth of the new freedom; 'a pattern, representing a river and a canal', the continuing flow of lives and the eternal dependence on nature, shaped and controlled by man; 'a jembe' or 'a pange', the tools of man's struggle and work. His final decision seems to contain a message of hope.

The struggle out of which Uhuru was born will be succeeded by a struggle no less bitter and confused in which men will again learn to shape the futures in their hands. Gikonyo decides that on his stool he will carve an image of birth.

He thought about the wedding gift, a stool carved from Muiri wood. I'll change the woman's figure. I shall carve a woman big-big with child. (p. 280)

Like birth the future can only be achieved through travail and endurance.

In the preface to *A Grain of Wheat* Ngugi describes his purpose as in part to show the effects of events which are 'real' - sometimes too painfully real for the peasants who fought the British yet who now see all that they fought for being put on one side . Although his novel ends with the events of Uhuru day it is clearly addressed to the generation which inherited its fruits, and contains an implicit warning of the abuse to which the new élite might subject the new order.

Immediately after independence the African writer was little inclined to question the new society created by the freedom struggle. As I have said, most of the writers addressed themselves to what Achebe had defined as the first task before them, to seek out and make articulate an African view of events long obscured by the bias of European myths of conquest and 'civilization'. Yet the period following independence was for many of them a period of bitter, personal disillusionment. In many places it became clear that the revolution had involved only a change of masters, and that the new black leadership had often taken over wholesale the privilege and isolation of the vacating colonial powers. The clear distinctions of the Independence struggle were replaced by more amorphous and more insidious problems, which were less easily grasped and less easily expressed. It seemed only natural and fair to many that the comfort and elegance of the white ruler should be appropriated by men like themselves. So the face in the Mercedes became a black face and the Presidential palaces were situated in the one-time fortresses of the slave traders. To the man in the street there was a kind of pride in the reflection that 'his own people' now owned and used these things. But, of course, this was a situation that could not last. When it became clear that the new ruling élite had no intention of distributing the new wealth fairly, and were often incapable of developing sources of fresh economic growth the stirrings of discontent began.

The writers were slow to respond to the new situation. Achebe's second novel *No Longer at Ease* (1960), set in the period of transition from colonial rule to full independence, initiated a series of attempts to define the problems facing a 'been to' who finds himself trapped between two sets of conflicting demands and who finally yields to the universal pressure to corruption. But its social criticism is limited, and a certain uneasiness is apparent, as if Achebe is a little unsure of what he thinks the novel is trying to say, and to whom. Its hero Obi is the grandson of the Okonkwo of *Things Fall Apart*. Achebe has recently said that he had originally planned to write an 'Okonkwo trilogy', in which the second novel would have been the story of Isaac-Nwoye, Okonkwo's son who abandons the tribe to become a Christian. Referring to the models for these figures, his own great-grandfather and father, he has said:

> There was something between those two that I find deeply moving and perplexing. And of their two generations – defectors and loyalists alike – there was something I have not been able to fathom. That was why the middle story in the Okonkwo trilogy as I originally projected it never got written ... in my gallery of ancestral heroes there is an empty place ...[20]

The recognition of the new task for the writer involves a recognition of the complicity he bears in the process by which the tribal world was destroyed and the new urban world brought into being. He is the lineal descendant of those defectors, like Isaac-Nwoye, who left the old ways to learn the new arts of the white man. Perhaps in *No Longer at Ease* Achebe, though working his way towards this realization, had not yet found the technique through which he could discover the full meaning of his place in the sequence, and the importance in his own definition of the role of that missing ancestor, Isaac-Nwoye. Whatever the cause, most critics have found *No Longer at Ease* a disappointing work, though it deserves recognition once again as a seminal novel whose subject-matter was to be taken up time and again by the new writers who followed.

It is this which makes Achebe such a central and compelling figure in the recent upsurge of writing in Africa. Not only is his work excellent in itself, but each step in his development initiated a new movement amongst other writers. In 1964 Achebe had said,

> I think I'm basically an ancestor worshipper ... Not in

the same sense as my grandfather would probably do it, you know, pouring palm wine on the floor for the ancestors ... With me it takes the form of celebration, and I feel a certain compulsion to do this. It's not because I think this will appeal to my readers, but because I think this is something that has to be done before I move on to the contemporary scene.[21]

With the publication of *A Man of the People* (1966) he moved on to the contemporary scene with new insight and vigour, and he has continued to do so through his first book of poems, *Beware, Soul Brother* (1972) and his first collection of short stories *Girls at War* (1972). In *A Man of the People* Achebe chooses, for the first time, to adopt a first-person narrative, and allow his story to emerge through the eyes of a young Nigerian, Odili Samalu. As in any first-person narration the meaning must be tempered by some attempt to establish the distance, if any, between narrator and author. Yet few critics have attempted to do this. It was Arthur Ravenscroft who first pointed out the need to read the book in the light of Odili's character and who warned that Odili is 'both serious accuser and comically self-accused in the rotten society of *A Man of the People*. It isn't simply a matter of contrast between Odili's word and his performance, but a question of how the words themselves reveal a shallow personality.'[22] *A Man of the People* interests as an absorbing, and even prophetic, account of the Nigerian scene post-Independence. But its continuing value will be as a novel in which technique and subject matter are welded together with skill and artistic judgement. In Odili Achebe has created a fascinating character whose very genuine idealism and moral indignation struggle continually with a personality which always sees the faults of those around him much more clearly than his own; and who is an adept in the subtle art of self-deception. Practically any of his speeches reveal this quality. For example, when first tempted by the specious but likeable Chief Nanga to visit him in the city he reflects that

> ... much as I wanted to go to Europe I wasn't going to sell my soul for it or beg anyone to help me. It was the Minister himself who came back to the post-graduate question at the end of his reception without any prompting whatever from me. (As a matter of fact I tried hard to avoid catching his attention again.) And the proposals he made didn't seem to me to be offensive in any way. He invited me to come and spend my holidays with him in the capital and while I was there he would try and find out from his Cabinet colleague, the Minister of Overseas Training, whether there was anything doing.[23]

The fundamental over-defensiveness, the slick phrasing and the subtle reinforcements ('the Minister *himself*') all work for an attentive reader to establish Odili's insecure plight.

The novel details the corruption which overcame the civil governments of Nigeria up to 1966, and which prepared the ground for the military coup in that year. In the portrait of Chief the Honourable M.A. Nanga M.P. the post-Independence politician is pinned firmly to the page like a gorgeous and over life-size butterfly. As the metaphor suggests Nanga is not without colour or charm. In fact a superabundance of these qualities is his very danger, as Odili discovers to his cost when he is sucked into his energetic wake. Nor are his virtues discontinuous with those of the people he represents. In many ways Nanga's success is directly attributable to the fact that, as the title suggests, he is really 'A Man of the People'. His characteristics, 'approachability', a catch-as-catch-can attitude, a philosophy which puts personal favours above abstract considerations are all sufficiently continuous with the traditional attitudes to make him seem to his electorate a man pre-eminently suited to his office. But, of course, Nanga is no longer an inhabitant of their world, and the values which in the semi-communal, intimate life of the village may sustain human affairs, in the life of the city become the buttress of a selfish, dog-eat-dog existence in which ideals cease to figure, and in which purpose is identical with personal survival. Thus the traditional village feeling that one ought not to enquire too deeply, or envy a man's success so long as others receive part of the gain ('You chop, Meself I chop, palaver finish.') becomes the tool of nepotism and bribery; while the semi-communistic philosophy of a theft not being a theft until one takes 'enough for the owner to see' becomes a cover for unbridled abuse and unprincipled public corruption.

In modern Nigeria the old world has not only been tamed, but put to work in the service of values diametrically opposite to those which it originally nurtured. In this world the Mask who once represented a vigorous and even dangerous threat to those who treated it lightly has been emasculated and tamed.

> While the Mask danced here and there brandishing an outsize matchet the restraining rope round his waist came undone. One might have expected this sudden access to freedom to be followed by a wild rampage and loss of life and property. But the Mask tamely put his matchet down, helped his disciples retie the rope, picked up his weapon again and resumed his dance. (p. 109)

Despite his early acceptance of Nanga's charity, Odili is gradually driven into opposition to him, though he is confused as to whether his motives are idealistic or personal, since Nanga has stolen away his girl-friend. He becomes involved with Max, a young opposition leader and fights Nanga's re-election. As the election progresses Odili is forced to come to terms with the fact that his own party is capable of actions which contradict his ethics, such as Max's acceptance of Nanga's bribe to withdraw as a source of funds for continuing the fight. But Odili's idealism is usually provoked by his pride as much as by moral purity, and soon he is reflecting that there is a personal slight in the fact that Nanga's bribe to Max was four times larger than that offered to him. Odili clearly develops in the course of the book, and he is no hypocrite. He does not consciously practice self-deception, and his idealism is quite genuine, as far as it goes. He often makes a courageous attempt to bridge the gap between his ideals and the shifting morass of standards which he discovers in himself, and in the world he has inherited. He sees more clearly by the end than anyone else in the novel what is wrong, but his perception is useless because by that time he shares too fully with those around him the very faults he perceives. He comes close to realizing this at an early stage when he reflects that

> The trouble with our new nation ... was that none of us had been indoors long enough to be able to say 'to hell with it'. We had all been in the rain together until yesterday. Then a handful of us – the smart and the lucky and hardly ever the best – had scrambled for the one shelter our former rulers left, and had taken it over and barricaded themselves in. And from within they sought to persuade the rest through numerous loudspeakers ... that all arguments should cease and the whole people speak with one voice ... (p. 42)

But despite such perceptiveness he is unable to act effectively and is left at the end of the novel with only a confused impression of what has gone wrong. His final conclusion, therefore, is bitter and inadequate.

> You died a good death if your life had inspired someone to come forward and shoot your murderer in the chest without asking to be paid. (p. 167)

Through the use of a narrator who is dissociated from the author Achebe is able to enter into the heart of the triviality, self-deception and bitter self-directed humour which is the only defence available to those who must live in the world of Nanga. The achievement of the novel is to discover a new technique, adapted to its material, which allows Achebe to practice the same objectivity which distinguishes his earlier novels. But as in the earlier novels objectivity does not mean coldness. Through the figure of Odili Achebe is able to analyze the problem with compassion and warmth. *A Man of the People* represents a new and compelling departure in Achebe's work, and looks forward to the new generation of novels which sought to articulate the disillusioned Africa of the late sixties.

SECTION 1—NOTES

1 MOORE, Gerald, *Seven African Writers*; Three Crowns; Oxford U.P., 1962; p. 39.
2 ACHEBE, Chinua, *Things Fall Apart*; Heinemann; London, 1959, p. 17.
3 SOYINKA, Wole, 'The Writer in a Modern African State' in Wastberg, Per (ed) *The Writer in Modern Africa*; Stockholm, 1968; p. 20.
4 ACHEBE, Chinua, *Arrow of God*; Heinemann; London, 1964. All quotes from African Writers Series edition; Heinemann; London, 1965.
5 POST, Kenneth, Foreword to Fawcett edition; Doubleday; New York, 1969; p. ix.
6 WALSH, William, *Commonwealth Literature*; Oxford U.P.; Oxford, 1973; p. 32.
7 AWOONOR, Kofi, 'Voyager and the Earth', *New Letters* Vol 40, No. 1; Autumn 1973, pp. 91-92.
8 MOORE, Gerald, 'English Words, African Lives', in *Présence Africaine*; No. 54; 1965; pp. 94-5.
9 NIVEN, Alistair, 'The Achievement of Elechi Amadi' in *Common Wealth* ed. A. Rutherford; (Akademisk Boghandel; Universitetsparken; Aarhus; Denmark, 1971; p. 94.)
10 NIVEN, Alistair p. 94.
11 NIVEN, Alistair p. 96.
12 AMADI, Elechi, *The Great Ponds*; Heinemann; London, 1969; p. 178.
13 NIVEN, Alistair p. 96.
14 Interview with Ngugi in *African Writers Talking* ed. Dennis Duerden and Cosmo Pieterse; Heinemann; London, 1972; p. 123.
15 See NGUGI, Wa Thiong'o, *Homecoming*; Heinemann; London, 1972.
16 NGUGI, Wa Thiong'o (James), *The River Between*; Heinemann; London, 1965; p. 164.
17 NGUGI, Wa Thiong'o (James), *Weep Not Child*; Heinemann; London, 1964, p. 43.

18 *African Writers Talking* (Interview with Ngugi).
19 NGUGI, Wa Thiong'o (James), *A Grain of Wheat*; Heinemann; London, 1967; p. 89.
20 ACHEBE, Chinua, 'Named for Victoria, Queen of England'; *New Letters*; Vol. 40, No. 1; Autumn, 1973; p. 17.
21 *Africa Report* No. ix; July, 1964; p. 20.
22 *Journal of Commonwealth Literature*; No. 6; January, 1969; p. 122.
23 ACHEBE, Chinua, *A Man of the People*; Heinemann; London, 1966; pp. 19-20.

2

CONFLICTS AND CONTINUITIES:
The African Writer and his Community

An important debate can now be seen to have emerged since the mid-sixties about the role of the writer in modern African society. In the early period the writer's initial tasks seemed clear, to assert the dignity and beauty of the cultures ignored or mutilated by colonial writers and historians and to support by this act the confidence and purpose of the newly independent nations. By the mid-sixties doubts and anxieties had begun to emerge, and a more satiric writing developed, and a novel like Achebe's *A Man of the People* catches the mood of this period. From this time onwards the debate begins to gather force.

In the early period a number of truths seemed self-evident and were generally accepted. The response of African writing in English would be rooted in the ideals of the independence struggles. The writer would be a teacher or guide, lending his skill to the education and direction of the masses. African writing, therefore, should avoid unnecessary obscurity. Specifically, it should draw on traditional forms and themes to make itself comprehensible to a people still only semi-literate, using English as a second language. These ideals led to an aesthetic which stressed the functionalism of African traditional art, its opposition to art 'for Art's sake'. Hopes ran high that the new vessels could be filled at the old wells, and that a style accommodating the structures of traditional forms to the English language would be a distinctive feature of English writing in Africa. The reports of the Conferences on African Literature and the Universities held at Freetown and Dakar in 1963[1] show as well as anything the hopes and doubts of the period. In his lecture on 'The Language of Poetry' Gerald Moore had asserted the impossibility of transliterating African poetic form into English. As he said, 'for my part I don't believe you can write French as though it were Wolof or English as though it were Yoruba'. In the discussion which followed the stress was on ways and means of accommodating African rhythms and language patterns to English. Significantly, nobody questioned the value of doing so if it were possible.

More recent discussions of these issues have had to recognize that two distinct streams of writing in English have emerged in Africa. The first directly stems from the concerns of that debate in Freetown, and seeks a way to develop a literature in English founded in the traditional aesthetic and responsive to its forms and structures; the second, more recent course has been the development of writers who, while drawing on traditional cultures for themes and images, see the function of the writer in a detached, post-modernist way and who are as willing to look to contemporary European or American models as to traditional African ones for the structural devices of their writing. This latter stance was always to some extent a feature of writing in South Africa, where labour policies and urban segregation led to a dislocation of traditional life and a model which shared as many features with black America as with black Africa. Examples of this can be seen from early writers like Peter Abrahams to later ones like Alex La Guma and Can Themba. Similarly the new writing in West and East Africa which shows these features has been pre-eminently concerned with the urban world; the much maligned early novels of Cyprian Ekwensi, for example or, more recently those of the Ghanaian writer Ayi Kwei Armah, and the Kenyan Meja Mwangi. The anonymous clerical hero of Armah's *The Beautyful Ones Are Not Yet Born* is essentially an inhabitant of the modern city, and whatever traditional roots he had have long withered away; similarly the young boys in Meja Mwangi's *Kill Me Quick* are unable to return to a rural life which has literally disappeared and are forced to seek an uneasy refuge in the more enduring if more destructive world of Nairobi.

This recent strain in African writing has had, naturally, a more immediate appeal for a European and American urban readership, and so perhaps the critical response to it has been overplayed. Ayi Kwei Armah's first novel was immediately hailed as a major contribution to African fiction. To most critics he seemed to emerge fully fledged, with a substantial technique and an assured point of view. As a result his subsequent novels were eagerly awaited, and despite a strong if flawed achievement in his second novel, *Fragments*, they have been rather disappointing. The initial enthusiasm was in response to those features calculated to appeal to a non-African audience: his careful symbolic structure; his precise and poetic use of metaphor and image; his existential questioning of identity and reality; and, above all, his concern with the survival of individual values in a corrupt universe. Naturally some of these very features irritated those African readers who held that African writing should develop its uniqueness out of traditional forms and concerns. Thus Kofi Awoonor, the poet and novelist, places Armah among those writers praised by non-African critics for bending their concerns to the European expectation and adopting the technique and 'role' of the European 'artist'. Awoonor points out that in this scale of appropriated European excellences

> The novels of Camara Laye are imitations of Kafka; Oyono is a rabid anti-white sensationalist; and the first true African novel was written by Yambo Ouloguem. The most authentic voice in fiction is Ayi Kwei Armah.[2]

The authenticity of Armah is, it seems, for Awoonor a sham and a parody. The 'universality' of his technique and themes are a weapon which European and American critics can use to beat down African structures and concerns. Thus, Armah belongs to that group of African writers who are praised by non-African readers for transcending 'narrow and parochial concerns of tribe and race because they sing of those things that all flesh is heir to'.[3] Whereas, as Awoonor implies, in reality their universality is only the mark of their irrelevance to African culture and their betrayal of the traditional function of the artist in African society.

Kofi Awoonor's lecture defines one of the poles in the debate over the African writer and his function in the seventies. His lecture is the clearest and most intelligent statement of the position which sees traditional African models as a continuing vital source of form and structure. It is all the more puzzling to discover that Awoonor's own literary work cannot be simply categorized according to his implicit model, as I will argue later. But his assertion gains force because he accompanies the criticism of his contemporaries with a positive definition of an alternative aesthetic model. He argues that,

> The traditional artist is both a technician and a visionary, these roles being indivisible and interdependent. His technical sense enables him to select and utilize materials which in themselves carry a spirituality, an innate essence. It is from here that the transformation into the visionary realm is primarily fed. Forms and motifs already exist, predetermined in an assimilated time and world construct. He only serves as an instrument for transforming these into an artistic whole, based on his imaginative and cognitive world, and upon a realizable principle of human joy, progress, and, more important, celebration. So he releases what for the non-artist could be regarded as the ambiguities, the complexities, and at times the paradoxes of the communal world, in the dynamic impulse of the details of his medium. In short, his art assays a reassemblement,

the establishment of a harmonic order. He is not a visionary person, like the European artist projecting into space and time structures which were not simply (sic) there before. There is no 'otherness' locked in a private psyche. Individually, of course, there are for him perplexing moments when form and motifs achieve a power over him, creating fear and apprehension. But he is ultimately restored to a community sensibility, to a resolution, a restoration of calm and quietude which alone is necessary for the widening of the human circle.[4]

It must be admitted that some of these phrases tell hard when we consider the work of a writer like Armah. His novels do often seem 'locked in a private psyche', and although they gain great unity and strength from being mediated through an individual mind struggling to understand his times, the anguish, bitterness and isolation of this figure has increased with each successive novel, so that his three novels sometimes seem staging posts along a road leading to personal obsession and despair. On the other hand the reader is left in little doubt of the genuineness of the writer's anguish.

What the criticism misses most, perhaps, is the fact that much of the writing it attacks is sustained not only by a personal vision, but also by an informed and deeply-felt political and social analysis which demands an honest and complete answer. As Gerald Moore has said,

> In Africa the writer will have to interpret his purposes to a society which refuses any romantic tolerance to those who isolate themselves from it, even for the sake of creative objectivity. It is precisely this problem of accommodation which lies at the heart of Ayi Kwei Armah's mordantly brilliant second novel *Fragments* ...[5]

When the African writer compounds this difficulty by mixing in unfashionable and unpalatable political truths he must expect even greater rejection and attack. This has certainly been the case with Armah. His refusal to compromise his stance and his outspoken commentary on the decay of revolutionary idealism in African society is not calculated to win him sympathy from those whose zeal is more effectively if more self-consciously maintained. In his third novel *Why Are We So Blest?* the significantly named narrator, Solo, reflects on his 'weakness' compared with those around him. Unlike him they seem serenely able to sustain the growing contradictions between assertion and truth in the politics of modern Africa.

> *They* are certain they are in a struggle that gives an answer to the ultimate why of life, making tomorrow's revolution. Their entrails have an iron toughness mine do not have. If they were ignorant, if they had no knowledge of what it is people call a revolution, or if they were all so young and so romantic as to know nothing of cracked promises and the maimed bodies of lost believers, but only about the adventure then I could also say of them: 'They will learn.' But they are not ignorant. They have learned as much about the things that have gone on and the things still going on as seeing eyes and hearing ears can teach anybody. Yet after all this knowledge, from somewhere within they find the enthusiasm to continue answering to the name of militants.[6]

One cannot help feeling that in the exchanges later in the same novel between Solo and Jorge Manuel, the representative of the exiled People's Union of Congheria, Armah is, at least in part, answering his real life critics in his own voice.

> 'For us, he said, 'the revolution takes precedence.'
> 'And for you the revolution doesn't raise personal prolems?'
> 'We all have personal problems,' he said, 'But it is egotism ...'
> 'That is not what I meant,' I interrupted him.
> 'Not egotism. Moral problems. Justice, for instance.'
> 'You interest yourself in abstractions,' he said.
> 'There are concrete problems. How to carry on.'
> I sensed we had parted company. (p. 53-4)

From the first Armah's novels have concerned themselves with figures who refuse to compromise their personal integrity and accommodate themselves to the decayed communal morality of 'You chop, meself I chop, palaver finish'. Whether the threat presents itself in the form of family pressure, as in *The Beautyful Ones*; the expectations of tradition grafted onto new forms of social demand, as in *Fragments*; or the obligation to be acceptably militant and *engagé*, as in *Why Are We So Blest*? Armah's central figures struggle to maintain a precarious grip on individual truth and personal meaning. Perhaps his critics are right, perhaps this is an essentially European obsession with individual vision, or an egotistic refusal to face harsh political realities, but it is certainly no easy road, since each of his heroes is finally beaten down to passivity if not acceptance. Whatever the limitations or dangers of Armah's aesthetic and political stance his novels represent a powerful and sustained view of the role of the artist and intellectual in modern Africa, a view which challenges complacency by its rigour and incisiveness.

I want to return to consider Armah's work in more detail later. But first I think we ought to be clear that the dispute about the work of writers like Armah is part of a wider concern with what one critic has characterized as the debate about obscurity and commitment in African writing.[7] Some writers and critics feel that in the context of the semi-literate state of most African countries the writer has a duty to make his points simply, and where possible in language and forms which forge connections with existing oral patterns in order to make comprehension simpler. This social critique is obviously inseparable from the aesthetic and cultural attitudes to the traditional art outlined above. Thus, the East African scholar Ali Mazrui has called for attempts 'to forge a connection with indigenous poetic traditions of folk tales, conversation and meaningful recounting of personal moments of experience' and concludes, 'Is poetry which is totally abstract as alien to Africa as is *laissez faire* liberalism or egotistical Protestantism? For the answer ... is an emphatic "Yes" ...'[8] Leaving aside the question of whether any such thing as a 'totally abstract' poem could be conceived let alone written let us be clear that Professor Mazrui is making an important point. As a political scientist he is well aware of the inseparability of culture and politics in modern Africa. He is aware, too, that the writer has a special role to play. His earlier work[9] makes it clear that he sees a separation of function between the writer as artist and the writer as citizen, but in his role of artist the writer has an obligation to communicate with his fellow-countrymen, many of whom have no way in to an understanding of poetry based on fractured, imagistic syntax and recondite allusions. Centring his attack by implication on the work of difficult and elusive writers like Christopher Okigbo, Mazrui compares their work unfavourably with traditional Swahili poetry where 'There are themes to follow, tales to tell. There is a concreteness of the whole rather than a mere solidity of parts'. Similarly in the lecture quoted earlier Kofi Awoonor attacks 'young Africans who speak with the tongues of T.S. Eliot, Pound, Hopkins – and of angels'.[10] But in an essay remarkable for its good sense and restraint Donatus I. Nwoga has pointed out that all African writers, whatever their stylistic stance, share a double tradition or, perhaps, a double exile:

> In the search for this new 'form and idiom' the modern African poet has two traditions in his background, the African poetic tradition and the poetic tradition of the language of his choice. And both of these traditions have problems which he must solve to achieve an individual style.[22]

Thus even poets like Kofi Awoonor (Songs of Sorrow), the Ugandan Okot p'Bitek (Song of Lawino, Song of Ocol etc;), or novelists like Gabriel Okara (*The Voice*) who seem to satisfy some of the demands made by Mazrui, can only translate the conceptual content of the traditional images. Much of the connotative force, to say nothing of the performance element of African traditional forms, is necessarily lost en route. Likewise even the most resolute modernists are engaged in describing and interpreting an African reality which shapes their themes and extends their borrowings in a unique way. The work of Christopher Okigbo is a splendid example of how a writer can work out of the whole range of effect and image available to the African writer using English. Thus in the early poem 'Heavensgate' he can create a passage like this

    DARK WATERS of the beginning.

    Rays, violet and short, piercing the gloom,
    foreshadow the fire that is dreamed of.

    Rainbow on far side, arched like boa bent to kill,
    foreshadows the rain that is dreamed of.

    Me to the orangery
    solitude invites
    a wagtail, to tell
    the tangled-wood-tale;
    a sunbird, to mourn
    a mother on a spray.
    Rain and sun in single combat;
    on one leg standing,
    in silence at the passage,
    the young bird at the passage.[12]

Here is a rich admixture of images drawing their force from traditional Ibo culture (the boa, the sunbird), from European mythology, literary allusion, and natural observation. If this early poem shows a certain separation of influences which makes the effect less than fully integrated, Okigbo quickly sharpens his skill. In the later sequence *Limits (3)* he moves through the wasteland of Eliot, the cultural relativism of Pound and back to the plight of the African poet he celebrates with an enviable ease and control.

BANKS of reed.
Mountains of broken bottles.

& *the mortar is not yet dry* ...
Silent the footfall,
Soft as cat's paw,
Sandalled in velvet in fur.

So we must go, eve-mist on shoulders,
Sun's dust of combat,
With brand burning out at hand-end.

& *the mortar is not yet dry* ...
Then we must sing, tongue-tied,
Without name or audience,
Making harmony among the branches.

And this is the crisis point
The twilight moment between
sleep and waking;
And voice that is reborn transpires,
Not thro' pores in the flesh,
But the soul's back-bone.

(*Labyrinths* p. 25 'Limits III')

There seems to be an unreasonable feeling on the part of some critics like Mazrui that Okigbo's use of European literary allusions is intrinsically wrong. One can see a certain force in the argument from social circumstances. But whether as an African poet he ought to have employed techniques which render him too obscure for a semi-literate audience is different from the issue of whether he uses these techniques successfully. And to this question I must give an emphatic, Yes. But, in addition, not only does the section above show a remarkably developed control of the various strands of the material, it also shows a sharp eye for the images and allusions relevant to his time and place. The residue of Eliot's

CONFLICT AND CONTINUITIES 59

wasted lives are as much in evidence in Enugu as in Antwerp, while Sigismondo Malatesta, so relevant to Pound as an archetype in a world where less gifted condottieri were busily acquiring their art collections, is no less relevant to a poet living in the acquisitive, coup-plagued world of modern Nigeria.[13]

Interestingly, in the final group of poems, the unfinished *Path of Thunder: poems prophesying war*, Okigbo was turning more and more to African sources for his allusions. In addition he was using rhythms which suggest the rhythms of traditional African poetry and developing a technique of building up poetry from existing units of sense which is a feature of some traditional oral forms. Thus in *Hurrah for Thunder* he uses these techniques to establish a satiric dimension which draws both on traditional satire forms and simultaneously echoes the Eliot of the 'Hurry Up Please Its Time' segment of *The Waste Land* and *The Hippopotamus*. Needless to say both echoing effects are now fully integrated factors in the structure. By this time Okigbo's verse has achieved a mature, individual and unmistakeable 'voice'. But it is an interesting hint of the openness of his mind that any and all contributory effects are welcome, a feature which characterised his poetry throughout his brief working career.

> WHATEVER happened to the elephant—
> Hurrah for thunder—
>
> The elephant, tetrarch of the jungle:
> With a wave of the hand
> He could pull four trees to the ground:
> His four mortar legs pounded the earth:
> Wherever they treaded,
> The grass was forbidden to be there.
> Alas! the elephant has fallen—
> Hurrah for thunder—
>
> But already the hunters are talking about pumpkins:

If they share the meat let them remember thunder.

The eye that looks down will surely see the nose;
The finger that fits should be used to pick the nose.

Today – for tomorrow, today becomes yesterday;
How many million promises can ever fill a basket ...

If I don't learn to shut my mouth I'll soon go to hell,
I, Okigbo, town-crier, together with my iron bell.
(Labyrinths p. 67 'Hurrah for Thunder')

Some of Okigbo's techniques in *Path of Thunder* recall Awoonor's structural devices in the poems which make up his *Songs of Sorrow*.[14] It is clear that in practice there is no simple division possible between the parties to the dispute about the form and purpose of modern African writing. Awoonor's poetry is intimately related to traditional form, and yet its structure retains many elements derived from European aesthetic models. Similarly as Okigbo's development shows, poets who sing with the tongues of Hopkins and Eliot may also be expert in more familiar poetic traditions. Nor is the communication argument of Mazrui as straightforward as it might appear to be. As Donatus I. Nwoga has argued, modern poets using traditional images and themes are not thereby automatically free from 'obscurity' for the ordinary African reader, since although their images may draw on familiar sources and structuring techniques they still assume a reader's ability to surmount 'a nearly unsurmountable problem to a mind restricted to the logical mode of poetic creation. (They) operate on the level of continuity of symbolic meaning, using images which on their literal level either make no meaning or even appear to conflict. Passages are constructed with the metaphors as their semantic constituents.'[15] The latter point is the most telling. As Ulli Beier's translations of traditional Yoruba poetry show the oral tradition is quite capable of handling images 'which appear to conflict', but the imagistic techniques by which a poet like Awoonor builds wholes out of these units are quite different from the structural techniques of oral traditions. Here, the eye follows the metaphor along the page, and the brain makes the connections. Nothing can prevent the page from infiltrating its distance and its self-consciousness.

The result, however, as in *Songs of Sorrow* is a poetry of great forcefulness which fully justifies Awoonor's hope that his poetry could catch 'the essence of these things' even if not 'in pure form' when rendered into English[16], and into print.

> Dzogbese Lisa has treated me thus
> It has led me among the sharps of the forest
> Returning is not possible
> And going forward is a great difficulty
> The affairs of this world are like the chameleon faeces
> Into which I have stepped
> When I clean it cannot go.
>
> I am on the world's extreme corner
> I am not sitting in the row with the eminent
> But those who are lucky
> Sit in the middle and forget
> I am on the world's extreme corner
> I can only go beyond and forget.
>
> My people, I have been somewhere.
> If I turn here, the rain beats me
> If I turn there the sun burns me
> The firewood of this world
> Is only for those who can take heart
> That is why not all can gather it.
> The world is not good for anybody
> But you are so happy with your fate;
> Alas! the travellers are back
> All covered with debt.   etc.[17]

It is difficult to do this poetry justice with excerpts, since as this segment shows the connections are made from each complete unit to the next, so that they form a continuous whole like a bead necklace, each bead single and yet all joined and interdependent in the whole. A similar, though less sophisticated, structural technique characterizes Okot p'Bitek's narrative poems[18], with the rider of course that the speaking voice of the central figure in each case provides a further unity.

However strong the desire to forge effective links between the contemporary world of the cities, dominated by an English-educated élite and the traditional sources of African culture in the rural villages the writers have not been able to ignore the fact that for nearly all of them education has placed them in the former world. Irrespective of their cultural and political attitudes their own histories have been largely that of the educated 'been-to', the natural consumers of the imported culture and the residual legatees of the white colonial élite. This is as true for a writer like Awoonor as it is for Armah. Both have written novels which explore the schizophrenic condition which this world produces in its inhabitants, and it may be instructive to compare their approaches.

For Ayi Kwei Armah the 'problem of accommodation,' as Gerald Moore has characterized it, is bound up with an increasing sense of personal futility as his heroes perceive the seamless web of corruption and decay into which the post-Independence world has woven the new goals and the old values. Although the traditional value systems persist they persist in altered and debased forms, and are often as potent a source of pressure and corruption as the new. For Armah then there is only a marginal comfort in the past. More than any other novelist in modern Africa his novels belong to an unremitting and persistent present, unacceptable and inescapable.

Fragments, his second novel, concerns itself with that ubiquitous West-African figure, the 'been-to', or man who has returned from education abroad. Through a pattern of defining images Armah sets out to explore the social and philosophical implications of his role in the community. The hero Baako Onipa struggles to retain his integrity as an artist, to maintain an objective and detached stance in a world where the artist is a form of civil servant, dependent on cultural grants and the sterile sinecure in the Ministry of Culture or the Broadcasting Commission. Such a stance is contradictory to all the demands made on the 'been-to' by his society and his family. Not only is the educated member of the new élite expected to maintain a suitable lifestyle (imported car, European suits, whiskies and soda etc ...) but, as Baako gradually realizes, he is also expected to fulfil obligations created by a dislocated and debased version of the old values of community and group economics. Struggling to come to terms with these demands he is forced gradually into catatonic withdrawal. As he strives to retain his grip on coherency he reflects that his role as 'been-to' has anthropological parallels in other cultures. In one sense he is the providing spirit, the bringer of goods, the expected cargo-carrier. He struggles to formulate his thoughts by writing them down, a solitary and incomprehensible exercise to his family, for whom expression must always be outward directed.

> ... hand go hand come. The been-to here then only fleshes out the pattern. He is the ghost in person returned to live among men, a powerful ghost understood to the extent that he behaves like a powerful ghost, cargo and all. Meets established, well-known expectations handsomely, *functions* like a ghost (look into Afro-American usage of word spook, also West Indian myth-clusters around the zombie idea), accepts the ghost role and feels perfectly at home in it. In many ways the been-to cum ghost is and has to be a transmission belt for cargo. Not a maker, but an intermediary. Making takes too long, the intermediary brings quick gains. The gaining circle is narrower, it is true, but with rockbottom realism inherent in the system the close ones find

nothing strange in it. It is life. The idea the ghost could be a maker, apart from being too slow-breaking to interest those intent on living as well as the system makes possible, could also have something of excessive pride in it. Maker, artist, but also maker, god. It is presumably a great enough thing for a man to rise to be an intermediary between other men and the gods. To think of being a maker oneself could be sheer, unforgiveable sin.[19]

Many writers have explored the effect on the returning African of the system of tribal and family obligations,[20] and the conflict which this sets up with the values and laws of a modern industrial society, but Armah's treatment is characterized by two distinctive features. Firstly, the degree to which Baako is isolated from African traditions by his education (a feature more commonly found in African novels in French, due to the 'assimilationist' educational policies of French colonialism e.g. Baako is quite isolated from the meaning of the rituals used to farewell him. No doubt the social accuracy of this will be questioned by some Anglophone African readers.) Secondly, by the political and economic analysis which Armah uses as the framework of his story, a framework which shows the consequences of the system for the whole economic life of West Africa. Here again a French influence is apparent and Armah, as in all his novels, draws heavily on the analysis of Fanon to drive home his comments on the unholy alliance of the old systems and the new and the essential unproductiveness of the emergent African middle class. For Armah the personal agony and disillusion of the hero is continuous with the decay inherent in the political and economic system of post-colonial society. This leads to the terrible sense of purposelessness and futility which pervades much of his writing. There is no possibility of singling out conscious villains. Even the corrupt new élite are victims, and the pressure on them to act as sterile transmitters rather than productive creaters is generated not only by their selfishness and greed but by the expectations of those they service. The potential innovaters are stifled, locked in a series of concentric small group demands, the family's, the village's and the tribe's, and so are barred from directing their power to solve the problems of the nation and people as a whole.

Fragments offers an unfashionable and uncomfortable view of modern West Africa. It refuses the usual categories and argues the complicity and venality of the populace at large in the destructive system. Such a view sits ill with many people; but their objections need to be coherent, for Armah's attack is made within a fully rendered political and historical framework and cannot be lightly ignored.

Armah's attitude to the traditional values is not dismissive. He recognizes their integrity and their value, but questions the uses to which they are put in the modern context. The book covers the viewpoint of three generations, and the dislocation occurs somewhere between them, though as the eldest, represented by his grandmother, recognizes, the historical source is much earlier in the divisive history of the slave trade when the people

> split their own seed and raised half against half, part selling part to hard-eyed buyers from beyond the horizon, breaking, buying, selling, gaining, spending ...
> (p. 284)

Naana, the grandmother, opens and closes the book with her reveries on the meaning of life and death. Waiting for death she literally occupies a ghost-haunted territory and so symbolically parallels the position of Baako the ghostly 'been-to'. Naana is a link with the effective communal world of the past. Its values are the same as those of her daughter in that she demands her share of the 'things of heavy earth' which the spirit-traveller is obliged to bring, but she recognizes that the process involves her obligations too, symbolized by the rituals which she struggles to maintain and which her daughter and son skimp and neglect. There is no nostalgia in Armah's treatment of Naana. Her world cannot be restored.

Its systems and patterns were effective and valuable, but they have been perverted into the modern myth of the 'shiny things' of consumer dreams. As Baako tells Juana, the Puerto Rican psychologist with whom he has an affair

> 'The myths are good here', he said. 'Only their use ...'
> His voice died. (p. 172)

For Armah traditional culture in modern Ghana is a trap used to prevent the individual from achieving creative independence. Thus the very words of the old rituals of mutual comfort and sustenance hint ironically at the forces which will destroy Baako.

> Do not be persuaded you will fill your stomach faster
> If you do not have others to fill
> There are no humans who walk this earth alone. (p. 6)

These rituals, which for Naana are 'perfect words, with nothing missing and nothing added that should not have been there ...' are employed by Baako's mother and his drunken Uncle Foli to justify parasitic dependence and uncreative consumption. Naana is blind to the full consequences of their attitude, and is content that by a trick she manages to outwit their self-centred meanness and give the spirits an adequate libation. 'The circle was not broken in any place. They will protect him.' How can she know that the circle has been surrounded and absorbed?

At the end of the novel Naana, dying, reflects on what she has known in her life, providing a commentary to define the experiences we have been shown against a completed cycle of life and history. In her age and blindness she parallels the crushed Baako, withdrawn and sightless in his catatonic isolation.

> From the world and the life around me, nothing comes to me. My eyes are no longer windows through the wall of my flesh but a part of this blinding skin itself. Soon

my ears too will be shut, and my soul within my body will be closed up, completely alone. (p. 278)

Both Baako and Naana are out of step with their time. For both of them the world is a series of discrete experiences and disunified acts. The old wholes have fallen apart and there are left only fragments making no vital connections, fragments which are used to batter and blackmail the survivors and dissenters. Baako's destruction has been accomplished by this process. He has been crushed by the tangled debris of decayed values, old and new; stoned into silence by the discarded pieces of his shattered inheritance. Naana's reflections make the process painfully clear:

> It is so vague, the way I think I see them sometimes; and they, I know, see me as nothing at all. The larger meaning which lent sense to every small thing and every momentary happening years and years ago has shattered into a thousand and thirty useless pieces. Things have passed which I have never seen whole, only broken and twisted against themselves. What remains of my days will be filled with more broken things ... another spirit has already found its death in the hot wet embrace of people who have forgotten that fruit is not a gathered gift of the instant but seed hidden in the earth and tended and waited for and allowed to grow – so busy have they become in their reaching after new things and newer ways to consume them. (p. 280-83)

The message of *Fragments* is a pessimistic one. There has been a darkening of vision in Armah's work since *The Beautyful Ones Are Not Yet Born* when the ending offered a muted hope and the possibilities of a better future. This trend has continued in Armah's horrifyingly graphic third novel *Why Are We So Blest?* in which the male figures are variously subject to destructive pressures from corrupt black political revolutionaries; American white bitch-goddesses in search of political purity and black stud service; sexually jealous racist *colons*;

and their own growing mental instability. In *Why Are We So Blest?* the threat seems to come from everywhere, within and without, and the enemy is variously: American puritanism; international aid programmes; white-black sexual myths; French and Portuguese colonialism; and corrupt black militancy. The novel clearly illustrates the dangers of personal obsession inherent in Armah's view, and only his superb structural sense prevents it from slipping over the edge into total paranoia. No doubt it will be used to justify attacks on his analysis of the role of the writer in Africa, so perhaps it is worth insisting again that despite the obsessive excesses of his latest novel, the first two novels constitute a reasoned and powerful statement of an important point of view. Whatever the weaknesses of his latest contribution he has defined a serious charge against the uses made of the romantic, anthropological view of African culture and shown the dangers inherent in this to the writer who insists on his detachment from the community he serves.

That way ... there was only annihilation

Superficially a reader is struck by the great similarity of theme and image between Awoonor's novel *This Earth, My Brother ...* and a novel like *Fragments*. Both deal with the disillusionment of young, educated Ghanaians and their search for meaning and purpose in their personal and public lives; both describe in graphic detail the sordidness and corruption of modern urban Ghana; and both have heroes who end their lives in a schizophrenic collapse, unable to cope with the contradictions and pressures of their situation. In view of the critical stance Awoonor has adopted towards Armah this may be puzzling. But a closer examination reveals radical differences in form and purpose. These differences confirm Awoonor's stated intentions to '(assay) a reassemblement, the establishment of a harmonic order' in the manner of the traditional artist. Although the novels examine the society of modern Ghana from the viewpoint of a troubled individual there is a wider context established in

CONFLICTS AND CONTINUITIES 69

Awoonor's work which refuses to allow the experience to remain 'locked in a private psyche'. Through image and motif he forces the reader to see the individual's plight as part of a continuous process, and so we view his ultimate destruction as a warning and a social indictment but not a symbol of inevitable despair.

This Earth, My Brother has a complex overlapping structure. It moves rapidly through present and past experience ordered in a series of more or less alternative chapters. The central figure, the lawyer Amamu, is a man of much the same background as Baako Onipa. 'A 'been-to' who has returned to Ghana, but who has, superficially, adapted to the system much more successfully. As his life-story unfolds in a series of flashbacks we gather information which places him in the world he inhabits. Estranged from his chic wife, a judge's daughter who spends most of her time abroad, he maintains the façade of his marriage while finding his emotional solace in his affair with Adisa, a night club girl whom he meets in court.

> There was a fight among the girls at the Lido. The police van came and took all of them to the station at Adabraka ... The next day they were hauled before the magistrate. She went to court in her working clothes, a red velvet low-necked frock that showed a quarter of her breasts ... He defended them. (p. 35)

The narrative ranges back and forth from his childhood as the son of a corrupt road overseer from the village of Deme to the seedy exclusiveness of the senior government drinking club where he hobnobs with his fellow men of power. There is no narrative structure, but each fragment adds to a picture of a man who is aware of having journeyed nowhere as he approaches middle age, and who is desperately in search of a lost assurance, variously symbolised by his village and by the Christian faith which directed and shaped his childhood education. The effect of these episodes is cumulative, and we begin to detect recurring preoccupations, e.g. the ironic paralleling of the lost Christian 'faith' and the loss of an

African faith, deeper and more vital, symbolized by the Dalosu-Yewe cult images. But some of the narrative material is over-extended and obvious. Thus, the picture of Deme Primary School which occupies all of Chapter Three is a rehash of conventional descriptions of the colonial education system, and colonial administration. The clichéd dialogue and internal monologues attributed to the young school inspector come straight from the pages of *The Wizard* or *Gem*.

> ...Washed up, that's what he is, washed up. You can't help liking the ass though. He was the spirit of every party. Has a lot of funny stories ... (p. 37)

And the mini-lectures which Awoonor delivers fit in poorly with the rendered action of the rest of the novel.

> The history of colonial education is one long war between the young and arrogant white school inspectors ... (p. 37)

Lapses like this are noticeable mainly because of the very effective structure in which they occur. The description of the Empire day parade in the same chapter is marred in the same way, though occasionally we see the kind of incisive and effective writing that Awoonor shows elsewhere in the novel.

> Meanwhile Deme and its surrounding villages waited for His Majesty's representative. Rule Britannia, Britannia rules the waves. The chiefs and people were gathered. Some came out of curiosity. They had finished planting the May crop. So if the white man was coming to talk some nonsense about a King far away, they might as well go and hear. When the moon is shining don't cripples hunger for a race? (p. 42)

Much of the narrative in the first half of the novel is a fairly conventional account of a colonial education, and if these sections were lifted out we would have an obvious and second-rate work. But they are embedded in a complex structure in which the reader is allowed to reflect on them in the context of the character's whole life as the novel moves from present to past to future action; to experience them against a counterpointing series of dream-like reveries in which the immediate significance is related to the subconscious world of dream and myth; and, finally, to forge both together as the reader becomes aware that what he is following is only partly the life of one man, and that the full significance of the events of the novel are only to be understood as a recreation of patterns which manifest themselves in individual lives but are not circumscribed by them. It is this complex structure which makes Awoonor's novel a poetic work of great power, and not just another account of the alienation imposed on the African by colonialism.

A series of reflective, reminiscent chapters are interposed between the sections of the narrative, which is itself arranged in flashbacks. Thus a double process of reviewing time present and time past is instituted, so that any event, public or private, is seen as part of a continuous flow of experience of which Amamu's life is only a portion. Thus Amamu's consciousness establishes the perspective on these events, but does not control them. The structure of this novel is far removed from the traditional European model in which narrative 'point of view' is the ordering principle. Here the narrator's point of view is only one of the events in an experience which lies outside any individual, even one who lives it. Awoonor is seeking in the novel to make good his claim that the modern African writer can adopt the stance of the traditional artist whose task is not to 'invent' but to continually 'rediscover' in the individual event 'Forms and motifs (which) already exist, predetermined in an assimilated time and world construct ...'[22]

In this sense the novel is profoundly experimental, seeking to discover a bridge between the causal and sequential demands of the European novel form, to which it must perforce bend, and quite different aesthetic principles which are inherent in the culture the form seeks to describe and probe. It is a fascinating and important statement of the problems involved in reconciling a European genre and an African cultural model.

The reflective chapters are loosely arranged as a series of memories covering much the same ground as the flash-backs with which they are interposed, and there is some evidence that the black notebook handed over to Amamu's parents at the end of the novel is a diary of these reflections kept by Amamu. But this barely developed explanation is only an irrelevant nod in the direction of conventional 'realism'. In practice the dream-like reflections are a psychic history which runs parallel to and deepens our understanding of the individual life recorded in the flash-back narrative chapters. Thus past events are reviewed both in the context of Amamu's individual life and in the context of the forces of which this is only a manifestation. Thus in an early section at the end of Chapter four (a reflective 'diary' chapter) we encounter a cluster of images which will recur in the 'real life' narrative, though not all related to the same person.

> I found her among the dancers sweating on the floor in one of those wild new dances of youth. She is my woman of the sea. She is the one who appeared through the cleft sea in the slash of the moonbeam to come to me under the Indian almond. She led me then through all farmlands, she led me over the wide lagoon where the sprats sang a song from the salt basins, over bird island we flew with the gulls returning from sea, over the sugar cane farms over the lagoon landing stage into the strange land, into Lave the forest of animals where we sat under my grandfather's blackberry tree as my uncle came with a smoked duiker caught in his trap as his dog Katsekpo jumped jumped like the District Commissioner's dog in the grass. She laughed revealing where the dentist removed her tooth while we chattered with the weaver birds overhead about old matters in boatlike nests in the market place. (p. 60)

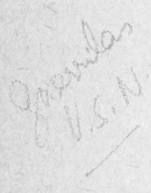

It is impossible here to unravel all the lines which radiate out from even a small passage like this. But the linking of the woman of the sea (a recurring figure intimately involved in the Ewe religious images in the book) with Adisa (Amamu's mistress) who also has a tooth removed, and with Alice (his wife) whose flashing teeth as she descends from the airplane bringing her back from England are described as 'pure and artificial' indicates how each of the women in Amamu's 'life' are both individuals and aspects of a figure whose significance as female deity has its roots beyond individual consciousness in the religious sources of his people. In fact Amamu's immediate relationship with the water-deity is through the Christian sect who worship on the beaches of his childhood, and whose converts, emerging dripping from the sea are, in their turn, manifestations of the ancient goddess. The cultural changes and the individual points of view are all aspects of a continuity which can be sensed only through symbol and image.

This goddess figure operates throughout the novel on many levels. But in one aspect at least she is that faith which Amamu has lost, and which he seeks to rediscover in his personal life through actions and people which the imagery reveals as only aspects of the real source for which he seeks. Thus Adisa, the mistress, whose 'skin was the darkness of silent northern rivers which do not dry up, though they are tributaries' (p. 111) and his long dead cousin Dede, his 'first love in the fields of wild flowers and butterflies long long ago' who 'came from the dead in the shape of the woman of the sea ...' (p. 57); even Alice, the cocktail party wife whose dress is adorned with 'patterns of dancing butterflies' (p. 125); are all aspects of a loss which is personal and yet communal, since Amamu's loss is ultimately of something beyond him which neither he nor any man can completely possess. It is for this reason that Amamu's defeat is not symbolic of the inevitable defeat of all men, but only of an aspect of life which he and all men must undergo now and always. As he reflects towards the end of the novel

So my woman of the sea was she that died in the death

of my cousin when we were young in the butterfly fields in infant days years ago when my prisoner butterfly fluttered and fled away perhaps to the land of my forefathers.(p. 145)

The novel takes up a very interesting stand on the social and political issues inherent in the theme. Whereas Armah's hero's defeat is set in a political context and implies the inevitable failure of a social idea, Awoonor's hero's defeat is seen as only superficially explicable by reference to the social conditions which 'cause' it. Amamu's loss of faith, and his isolation from the sources of his identity are the product of the colonial education system, of the missionaries, of the economic exploitation of the British and the black élite who take over from them, but this in its turn is only symptomatic of a larger failure which viewed thus is part of the human plight. It is to be fought against and struggled with, but it is not a cause for despair. The African failure is no more inherent or inevitable than any other human failure. Awoonor is sharply aware that indictments such as Armah's are in part acted out in response to European and American demands that Africa and Africans demonstrate and prove the worth of their societies and cultures. The search to recover an African culture presupposes that it has been lost, and Awoonor seeks to show that its 'loss' is often established by references which are irrelevant to it. The lost African culture the would-be revivalists seek to rediscover is, in part, a projection of European fantasies. The African Culture they seek is as fictional as the European Culture they have adopted

> ... He drove past the Institute of Arts and Culture where a crazy group of drummers and artists and their leaders were reviving African culture with a vengeance every day. On his left were the temporary buildings of the National Lottery ... (p. 19)

The juxtaposition speaks volumes.

For Awoonor the scramble to create an African culture too often means the scramble to 'create' a culture which can be translated into forms comprehensible to European aesthetics. In a devastating image Awoonor sums up the paradox at the heart of the search for an acceptable African identity, a praiseworthy mulatto culture.

> What has Africa to contribute to the world? asked the learned professor.
> If you have no history create one, if you have no culture, invent one, for the question is being asked and, brother, you must come forth with an answer, pronto. She fell madly in love with a Swiss gentleman. Secretly she wanted a mulatto baby, fair with long hair. The species must be improved. They have stayed black for too long and black is not beautiful. Her mother and her aunts in Cape Coast screamed over the baby. What a beautiful baby, and named her She Who Was Born in the White Man's Country. (p. 134)

This is not to say that he is not aware of the destructive losses caused by colonial history, nor that he fails to see the gap between promise and performance in modern African society. His descriptions of the corruption and pettiness of many aspects of modern Ghanaian society are as pointed and sharp as any of his contemporaries. But he clearly feels that more is required in response than a policy which seeks to define success as synonymous with European and American approval for 'improvement' along their projected models. In contrast, an honest appraisal involves an awareness that, ultimately, nothing is lost and that the modern African is, for better or worse, a product of all the forces which have shaped him. Nothing less than this is adequate ground on which to build a response.

> The world will be emptied of matter, a prognostication shall be offered by hoary-headed elders under nim trees pipes in their mouths lamenting the many unmentionable sins committed by present day youth against tradition. The classical gentleman, well read in Herodo-

tus at Cambridge, shall solve the educational problems of Africa by a document that must have its preamble in Latin and be larded with quotations from Heraclitus.

For childhood shall end here upon these estatic shores where a renewal of faith shall be achieved by the sacrificing of our manhood's innocence, for as the Leader said, we, the Africans, must be jet propelled into the twentieth century.

For this earth, my brother, shall claim you for her own ... (p. 134)

What Awoonor has sought to do, it seems to me, is to develop a structure which suggests that continuity of the overlapping strands which make up the life of an individual or a people. In so doing he denies both the romantic anthropological view of man which leads to a projected African identity obtainable only by a process of drastic exclusion and distillation, and the despairing view of a writer like Armah to whom alienation is inescapable since product and process are identical and so inevitably linked. *This Earth, My Brother* ... is an attempt to *celebrate* continuity. At first, this may seem difficult to reconcile with Amamu's fate, since at the end of the novel he despairingly flees back to his childhood home from where he is led away in a catatonic state. But Awoonor's point is his refusal to allow the personal experience of Amamu to surround the structure of events which has produced it. Thus the multiplicity of possibilities both past and future are not rendered futile by Amamu's failure, as they are with Armah's Baako. For Awoonor the individual psyche is not the ultimate viewpoint on the reality the novel explores. Reality exists outside and beyond the men who struggle to comprehend it and failing, die. In this sense Achebe's Ezeulu was reintegrated in the moment of his defeat. So Amamu is reintegrated at the moment of his defeat on the beach at Deme.

> Then slowly he saw her, the woman of the sea, his cousin love of those years long long ago rising from the sea ... It

seemed suddenly that the centuries and the years of pain of which he was the inheritor, and the woes for which he was singled out to be the carrier and the sacrifice, were being rolled away, were being faded in that emergence. Here at last, he realized with a certain boyish joy, was the hour of his salvation. It was coming at last. She rose now up upon the waves, her breasts bare, her nipples blacker than ever. On her face a little smile; the sun gave out a radiance that recalled the bright sunshine of the butterfly fields and the hunt of childhood and her first epiphany. (p. 179)

Individual experience must be fitted into a pattern of past, present and future which is continuous beyond reference to the individual. It is into this pattern which the plight of the present must be fitted, and against this pattern defeat and victory measured. As Awoonor has said against this perspective the man and the artist can fit his 'fear and apprehension' and can be 'ultimately restored to a community sensibility, to a resolution, a restoration of calm and quietude which alone is necessary for the widening of the human circle.'[23] The perplexities and apprehensions of the modern African artist must far outweigh those of the traditional artist, subject as he is to demands which are so much more violent and contradictory. But from the traditional aesthetic he derives the goal to which Awoonor still wishes the African artist to direct himself, the goal of reconciliation to and celebration of the human spirit.

SECTION 2—NOTES

1 MOORE, Gerald, *African Literature and the Universities*; Ibadan University Press; Ibadan, 1965.
2 AWOONOR, Kofi 'Voyager and the Earth'; *New Letters*; University of Missouri – Kansas City; Vol. 40 No. 1; Autumn, 1973; pp. 87-8.
3 AWOONOR, 'Voyager and the Earth'; p. 87.
4 AWOONOR, 'Voyager and the Earth' pp. 89-91.

5   MOORE, Gerald, 'The Writer and the Cargo Cult' in *Common Wealth* ed. Anna Rutherford; Aarhus U.P.; Aarhus, 1971; p. 73.
6   ARMAH, Ayi Kwei, *Why Are We So Blest?*; Doubleday; New York, 1972; p. 13.
7   NWOGA, Donatus I., 'Obscurity and Commitment in Modern African Poetry'; *African Literature Today* No. 6; Heinemann; London, 1973; pp. 26-45.
8   MAZRUI, Ali, 'Abstract Verse and African Tradition'; Zuka; 1; Sept. 1967, pp. 47-9.
9   I am thinking of Mazrui's fictionalized polemic *The Trial of Christopher Okigbo*; Heinemann; London, 1971.
10 AWOONOR, 'Voyager and the Earth'; p. 87.
11 NWOGA, 'Obscurity and Commitment'; p. 31.
12 OKIGBO, Christopher, *Labyrinths – Poems*; Heinemann; London, 1971; p. 4.
13 Pound's reference to Malatesta is in Canto VIII, which Okigbo echoes in the refrain. See EGUDU, Romanus 'Defence of Culture in the Poetry of Christopher Okigbo'; *African Literature Today* No. 6; Heinemann; London, 1973; p. 22.
14 See *Rediscovery and Other Poems*; Mbari Publications Ibadan, 1964. Also *Modern Poetry from Africa* ed. Moore and Beier; Penguin; London, 1963.
15 NWOGA, 'Obscurity and Commitment'; p. 37.
16 MOORE, *African Literature and the Universities*; p. 114.
17 MOORE and BEIER, *Modern Poetry from Africa*; p. 98. Note: In this anthology Awoonor is listed as George Awoonor-Williams.
18 p'BITEK, Okot, *Song of Lawino* (1966), *Song of Ocol* (1970); East African Publishing House; Nairobi.
19 ARMAH, Ayi Kwei, *Fragments*; Houghton and Mifflin; Boston, 1970; pp. 224-5.
20 E.g. Achebe's *No Longer at Ease*; Soyinka's *The Interpreters*; Cheik Hamidou Kane's *Ambiguous Adventure* (French) and Ama Ata Aidoo's *The Dilemma of a Ghost* (play) which employs a cluster of similar 'ghost' images.
21 AWOONOR, Kofi, *This Earth, My Brother*; Heinemann; London, 1971.
22 AWOONOR, 'Voyager and the Earth' pp. 90-91. Quoted above.
23 AWOONOR, 'Voyager and the Earth'; pp. 90-91.

3

CHILDHOOD AND LEAVETAKING:
Growing Up in the Caribbean

If the African writer in the twentieth century has been concerned with questions of identity and place, and has suffered a double exile from his own tradition and from that which he has been offered by education and colonial example, the West Indian writer has suffered these same problems with an added intensity. The African writer has an alternative, living tradition to that offered by his schooling; a language which he possesses by birthright; and an historical identification with the continent he inhabits. The West Indian has only the fact of his separate existence, his colour, and his distinctive habits to oppose to the colonial values he has inherited. It is not surprising then that the central fact of West Indian writing is the struggle to define a separate West Indian reality and to establish its values as significant and worthwhile. The African was colonized, the West Indian was enslaved. In the process of enslavement the West Indian was deprived of his personality, as well as his roots and his cultural identity. All that he can begin with is his own experience. Perhaps for this reason the West Indian novel has been especially rich in accounts of childhood and adolescence, tracing the individual's journey to consciousness and his struggle to understand himself and the world he lives in. As Victor Ramraj has said, in a very real sense, 'The

West Indies that the Caribbean child discovers is himself.'[1]

In the introduction to his short stories *Cricket in the Road* the Trinidadian writer Michael Anthony describes his motives in starting to write.

> I wrote ... with the idea of seeing if I could tell a story I wanted to tell by mixing fact with fiction ... It seemed to me that a work of fiction based on fact was more meaningful than one that stemmed totally from the imagination. I felt that even if the people directly concerned are dead, the story has some historical significance, especially if it is linked to some recognizable place.[2]

Here Anthony is responding to the need of the West Indian writer to define his roots, and to come to terms with his own time and place. For the West Indian the world which lies about him from childhood upwards is filtered through a set of alien images, actively fostered by an educational system which renders it unreal and fictional. What is lost in this filtering process is not only an individual pride in identity and a sense of place, but any historical consciousness of what it means to be a West Indian. Without this sense of identity and place there can be no development of a racial and cultural inheritance. The cultural patterns imported from England to the West Indies and carefully fostered to supplant any existing African, Indian or Asian patterns were designed to perpetuate a status quo in which the 'native' was taught to despise himself and to see his advancement in terms of the successful imitation of his English masters. The more successful he became in this endeavour the more he was alienated from his own people, and the more dependent he became on the English ruling class who retained the reality of power. The upward limit of his own social mobility was clearly defined to include only the trappings of power, to create an 'overseer' class. For a West Indian writer like George Lamming the new post-Independence rulers are only the final representatives of this class of middle men.

> Alienated by the psychological demands of their education from the masses below them ... exiled from the regional peaks of the economy ... while other men, in no way superior to them in fact or potential, give the ultimate directives about petroleum and bauxite and sugar. Here is a humiliation that goes deep ...[3]

This alienation was deliberately fostered by an educational system designed to maintain and reinforce the colonial status quo. As Lamming has said the West Indian, stunned and disorientated by the horrors of the Middle Passage, deliberately discouraged under the slave laws from preserving more than fragments of his own culture, was ripe to be seduced into accepting as his own a value system profoundly opposed to his needs and totally alien to his tradition and race.

> This human diversity encountered itself in a state of original isolation; isolated, that is, by the lack of a common idiom, and imprisoned by orders which were absolute. And most important of all, these were orders given in a language the people could not understand ... isolated by a lack of common idiom, this humanity made a bid for possession of the language, exposed utterly and naked to the process of being possessed by all the conceptual and poetic possibilities of the language that would become their new possession. Supervising this complexity of learning to be a new man, in a new place, was an authority whose home was elsewhere ...[4]

With such material to work upon the colonial education system was easily able to direct its aspiring pupils into an imitation of the values of their masters and an attitude of distaste and rejection towards those retained or developed in the Caribbean. History and achievement was English, poetry was Wordsworthian splendours in the grass, and human endeavour and pride was something which happened elsewhere. In Lamming's novel *In the Castle of My Skin* the process is made clear. The school is presented as the literal extension of the slave ship:

> There were nine squads comprising about a thousand boys. The squads were packed close, and seen from the school porch the spectacle was that of an enormous ship whose cargo had been packed in boxes and set on the deck ...[5]

A ship which with ironic cruelty is pretending to be on course to a land where they can be part of the flow of events which they study, where they can make history.

> Fourth Boy: We going to make his'try. I always want to make some hist'ry.
>
> Second Boy: Me too. I read 'bout all those who been making hist'ry, William the Conqueror an' Richard an' all these. I read how they make hist'ry, an' I say to myself 'tis time I make some too.
>
> First Boy: We going to make hist'ry by Foster Fence. Let's make hist'ry. (p. 48)

The irony of the last comment is limited to its internal function in the passage. There is nothing intrinsically ironic about making history 'by Foster Fence'. What prevents its possibility is not some innate quality of the place but the view that its inhabitants have been taught to hold of it. Thus the boys can not really see the meaningfulness of Foster Fence or any of the places around them because they have no historical context in which to place them. They have been taught the history of Sussex lanes, and Yorkshire dales but not of the islands they inhabit. They have learned of the great events which shaped their masters' fate but know nothing of their own people's past. Thus, for example, slavery, the central shaping fact of the West Indian reality is a mythic event to them.

> They had read about the Battle of Hastings and William the Conqueror. That happened so many hundred years ago. And slavery was thousands of years before that. It was too far back for anyone to worry about teaching it as history. That's really why it wasn't

taught. It was too far back ... Probably it never happened at all. (p. 58)

In the Castle of My Skin exposes the lie at the heart of the colonial educational myth, that nothing happened in the West Indies. It shows that this is only true if we accept the perspectives of a ruling European élite whose interests were served by teaching this lie as truth. And it further shows, in the figure of the school teacher Mr. Slime, how the first generation of popular leaders were won over to support the structure on which the lie was erected by being bribed with the droppings from massa's table. If nothing happened in the West Indies in the eighteenth and nineteenth centuries, then, it was because the colonial powers did not dare to allow it to happen. The only meaningful historical action a slave can take is to revolt. Thus from a European viewpoint the history of the West Indies during the colonial period is simply a succession of balance sheets punctuated by bloody and unsuccessful slave insurrections. West Indians themselves were led to accept this view, and to conclude that they had no history. Though reflection would indicate that the cause of this state of affairs was the policies and attitudes of the European rulers. Yet, ironically, it is this imposed state of deprivation which West Indians have been taught to regard as a matter of shame and a proof of their innate inferiority. Thus even a perceptive and curious writer like V.S. Naipaul seems to accept a West Indian responsibility for the futility he discovers in the West Indies and its history,

> ... History is built around achievement and creation; and nothing was created in the West Indies ...

and, implicitly, to blame this futility on the pettiness and self-lacerating snobbery of the West Indians themselves. But, as Lamming has argued, the West Indian was never offered an alternative except as a carrot to entice him into mutual jealousy and self-betrayal. Colonial educational policies were directed towards the suppression of a sense of identity. As Trumper tells G. in *In the Castle of My Skin*

None o' you here on this islan' know what it mean to fin' race. An' the white people you have to deal with won't ever let you know ... (p. 295)

The West Indies, as Lamming sees it, is the supremely successful instance of British colonial administration. West Indians were made to feel guilty and ashamed of their 'failure' to achieve mythical 'English' standards which they could never really attain, and which militated against the development of traditions and values of their own. This situation led to the central importance in West Indian writing of the idea that the West Indian world is fictional and unreal. As long as the perceiver remains within that world he sees it in the terms he has been taught. Although his emotions assure him of the reality of his experience, and his mind tells him that its values are as real as any other, the prejudices of generations still whisper that at best such experience and such values are a minor offshoot of the 'real thing'. Paradoxically, the real world is that which percolates down to him through the fictions of books, magazines and foreign newspapers, while his actual surroundings are shadowy because they do not resemble the archetypes to which he has been conditioned to respond. The importance of language in this process, as Lamming saw, cannot be overstressed. No words, no structures or forms were available to establish the West Indian reality. These are what the West Indian writer had to create, and create for himself.

Michael Anthony in his short story *Sandra Street* catches the agony and pathos of this situation by going inside the West Indian child's struggle with the task of perceiving and recording the world he lives in.

The boy Steve who comes from Sandra Street, an isolated half-rural straggle of houses that marks the division of town and bush, obscurely feels that Sandra Street has a unique and valuable character. But he is unable to defend it in terms of the values which prevail on the 'other side of town'. Kenneth the town boy, can easily put Sandra Street in its place. In his school essay on the subject he writes:

> Sandra Street is dull and uninteresting ... I do not think it is a part of our town at all because it is so far and different from our other streets.[7]

Obscurely Steve feels that something has been left out of this judgement but he doesn't know what it is. Defensively, he reflects:

> Yet the boy's composition was truthful. Sandra Street was so different from the other streets beyond. Indeed, it came from the very fringes and ran straight up to the forests. As it left the town there were a few houses and shops along it, and then the school, and after that there were not many more houses, and the big trees started from there until the road trailed off to the river that bordered the forests. (p. 10)

The teacher Mr. Blades sees the boy's dilemma and points out to him the need to look at Sandra Street and capture its reality with the same force that he can capture the more accessible experience of the town. He draws his attention to the unique features of the street, and admonishes him gently:

> 'You noticed all this and you wrote about Sandra Street without mentioning it, eh? How many marks did I give you?'
> 'Forty-five.'
> He looked surprised. 'I gave you forty-five for writing about the noises and about the dirty trams of the town? Look.' he pointed, 'Do you see?'
>   'Mango blossoms,' I said, and I felt like crying out: '*I wanted to show it to you!*' (p. 14)

The story culminates with Steve's taking Mr. Blade to see the bananas which he has placed in the roots of an immortelle to ripen. He had mentioned them in a later 'composition'. As they both stand among the hills looking out over Sandra Street the boy is puzzled by the intensity of Mr. Blade's reaction.

'Sir,' I said in happy surprise, after removing the covering of trash from the bunch. Mr. Blades was gazing across the trees. I raised my eyes. Not far below, Sandra Street swept by, bathed in light.

'The bananas, sir,' I said.

'*Bananas!*' he cried, despairingly. 'Bananas are all you see around you, Steve?'

I was puzzled. I thought it was for bananas that we had come to the hills.

'Good heavens!' he said with bitterness. 'To think that you instead of Kenneth should belong to Sandra Street.' (p. 18)

In this brief, unvarnished tale Anthony has put his finger squarely on the dilemma of the young West Indian. His education has directed him away from that which he is uniquely qualified to understand. He has been literally blinded to his own inheritance. In its place the West Indian child is offered English culture via English literature. Yet, as V.S. Naipaul has shown, he has no means of really grasping this. If he is imaginatively to make it his own he must adapt it to fit a tropical, alien experience. The result is that this literary experience remains sunk in the taint of fantasy. Describing his reaction to Dickens's characters, Naipaul has written

> I gave them the faces and voices of people I knew and set them in buildings and streets I knew (in Trinidad). The process of adaptation was automatic and continuous. Dickens's rain and drizzle I turned into tropical downpours: the snow and fog I accepted like conventions in books.

Trapped in this way between a present reality for which he has no models and a set of models which do not fit his reality the West Indian writer has, naturally, turned inwards to examine the growth of his own perception and its characteristic modes. Just as with the African writer, though with even more radical cause, the autobiographical novel, the novel of childhood and departure has been not only a summing up of experience past but also an attempt to define the way ahead. Before we can act it is necessary to know who we are.

In a recent lecture Victor Ramraj has commented on the wide range of West Indian novels and stories dealing with childhood experience. Writers who have dealt with childhood, or used a child narrator, include not only Lamming and Anthony but Andrew Salkey, Austin Clarke, Ian MacDonald, V.S. Naipaul and Christopher Drayton. The range and diversity of interest in childhood experience indicates to Ramraj that

> The child can play a part in the emergent West Indian literature ... because in a culture seeking independence, the child enjoys a natural if precarious enfranchisement. He provides a fresh point of view; a Gulliver without fantasy, a Christopher Columbus of the present exploring the islands of manhood, remaking the maps.[8]

By recreating the experience of childhood the novelist can literally trace the growth of a specific West Indian consciousness, and show how it is shaped into a unique and distinctive pattern by the social, political and geographical realities it encounters. The Trinidadian novelist Michael Anthony stands out in any discussion of the novel of childhood in the West Indies. His three published novels, and his collection of short stories all deal with childhood experience. Anthony's peculiar skill is to be able to recreate the unmediated experience of the child, allowing the reader to share the actual shaping of responses as they occur. Other writers, notably Andrew Salkey in his children's novels, have 'gone behind' the child with skill and sensitivity, but no one has gone further than Anthony towards recreating the actual experience of growing up in the West Indies. His second novel *The Year in San Fernando*[9] will undoubtedly be recognized one day as a minor classic. In the novel Anthony traces a year in the life of a twelve-year old Trinidadian boy from a rural village who comes to the town to spend a year as companion to an old lady, Mrs. Chandles. It is no part of Anthony's purpose to document Trinidadian life, nor to comment on the social and political forces at work in it. But as we view the world through Francis's eyes we build up a detailed and authentic picture of Trinidadian social divisions, family patterns, economic conditions and cultural expectations, all revealed not as abstractions but as they shape themselves in the awareness of the child who grows up with them. Our awareness of this world grows along with that of Francis. During the course of a brief twelve months we are shown the gradual broadening of his perception, not in any spectacular way but as a slow process of adjustment to confusing and sometimes contradictory experiences. Since Francis is too young to influence his surroundings he has to grow with them, and so edges toward a comprehension of the realities of the world outside his village and the adult life it represents.

The centre of the novel is the changing relationship between Francis and Mrs. Chandles, who continually finds fault with him and neglects to feed him properly, and whom, at first, he regards as a tyrant and a bully. As his experience widens and he is able more accurately to judge the motives of those around him, his feelings towards the old woman gradually change. A passage of simple reportage can capture such a moment of change, recording the actual growing point of Francis's comprehension.

> I knew she was happy because of the rains. She had said, 'God! look at this weather!' but I knew she was pleased about it. She was not even angry about my coming into the house with dripping clothes ... Anytime now I expected her to say this was the worse rains she had seen. I waited, almost amused, to hear that. She moved about the kitchen with zeal. I looked at her. (p. 107)

At this moment Francis realizes, and we along with him, that Mrs. Chandles's short temper and anger is not the result of an evil disposition but of the discomfort of a neglected old woman in a dry season waiting for rain. If Francis's personal understanding is deepened by his experience at San Fernando, so is his social awareness. But again, the novel does not impose a false adult perceptiveness on the child. He records discrepancies as he comes across them, and lays down a history of actions which will be the foundation of later discriminations; but there is no authorial manipulation of these events to flatter the political or social consciousness of the reader. Thus, when Francis first comes to the house of the Chandles it seems a palace, totally unrelated to his home. But, as he grows more familiar with its wonders, his mind is able to accommodate the two in a continuous vision which is the beginning of comparison and criticism.

> I went on thinking of the pressure lamp in a sort of way. In the town there was still a number of houses with lamps but by far the majority of houses had electricity. There was electric street-lighting also and some streets were lit up all through the night.
>
> There was no such thing as electricity at Mayaro. Not a single house had that. And as for the pressure-lamps, only two houses had this – the Forestry Office, and the doctor's home. You could see the doctor and Mrs. Samuels were proud about this and they felt they were very modern. And they were too, considering. (pp. 76-77)

Francis's mind is open to experience in a direct and immediate way. His own reflections emphasize that he is not conscious of reasons for the change in his feelings towards Mrs. Chandles, towards her sons, or towards San Fernando itself. As a child he measures the world by his immediate response, not by his motives for that response, which often remain mysterious and unknown.

> I could feel it there between us. I could feel it strong and real ... I wondered when did all this start up, because it wasn't sudden ... inside me I was feeling new. (p. 170)

The illness which has been growing on Mrs. Chandles

throughout the novel culminates with her death just before Francis is due to leave. The year he has spent in San Fernando is marked by a cumulative series of losses which are linked together in the boy's reflections. The journey itself is his first severing of the links of the family; the departure of Brinetta, Mrs. Chandles's first home help, to her unknown village, a second puzzling encounter and departure; while Mrs. Chandles's death is his first intimate contact with the inevitable ending that is part of the life he is about to enter. As the novel draws to an end he reflects on how the year at San Fernando has involved him. But even here the experience remains fragmentary and half-digested, the raw material of perception not a finished product.

> I remembered the mountain and suddenly I looked back but all the windows were closed because of the rains. The bus roared on and my mind went on Mrs. Chandles, who was dying, and Mr. Chandles – so strange of late, and now homeless; and that dollar – I thought of all the mixed-up things, of all the funny things, in fact, which made the year at Romaine Street. (pp. 183-4)

Francis has changed in the course of his year. He has encountered a new world and adjusted to it. His perceptions have altered, too, as his changed recollections show. Speeding homeward through the same outskirts which had so impressed him on his way to San Fernando he reflects that

> Here the place was really different and the houses were not one beside the other now but in places very widely apart. They were older and unpainted and there were no fences around them and they looked free in the big spaces. I could not remember these parts at all. (p. 183)

Mayaro, too, will have changed when he returns, as will his brothers and sisters. His mother, as he had noted on her visit, already looks changed to him.

> I noticed that her face was a little more sunken, so her

cheek-bones stood out. Her head, very full of hair, surprised me because I had not remembered so much grey upon it. (p. 82)

Anthony's purpose is not to establish an ironic distance between the reader and Francis. There is no attempt to create a superior tone with which the reader may identify against the 'innocent' and inexperienced vision of Francis. Of course, the reader is made aware of significances which remain hazy and incoherent in the child's mind, but he is also made aware that 'judgements' of this kind are not the novel's primary concern. What Anthony seeks to do is to draw the reader into sharing Francis's experience. We are forced to shed our own preconceptions as we engage with Francis's attempt to discover the meaning of the world he encounters. As a result we respond to this world as fully and openly as the boy himself, shedding in the process our existing prejudices, and learning to understand how he is being shaped by his experience. The Trinidadian reality is revealed as it forms itself in the consciousness of the boy. For the first time, perhaps, we are striving to live inside this world.

George Lamming sees the rise of the novel as providing for the first time 'a way of investigating and projecting the inner experience of the West Indian community'. For Lamming the resulting self-awareness is as important an event in West Indian history as the discovery of the islands, or the abolition of slavery and the influx of Asian labour in the nineteenth century. Even African writers have not seen their work as being so crucial, perhaps because for them the task was, in part, to recover and revitalize their own cultures. For the West Indian writer the task is to help create that distinctive culture. Through personal history the writer can seek to distinguish the unique influences and conditions which have shaped the modern West Indian experience. Lamming's *In the Castle of My Skin* traces the events in the life of G., its boy narrator, from his ninth birthday until he leaves Barbados as a young man. As a boy his world is defined entirely by his village, a village owned by and named after, its white owner Mr. Creighton. Through the story of his childhood we are shown a picture of the village and the complex social pattern in which peasant, overseer and landlord are bound together. The characters span the whole gamut of age and the whole social perspective.

Ma and Pa, the two oldest inhabitants, wait for death with a philosophic resignation. The boy's mother is alone, as are most of the mothers of his friends, a situation brought about by a social system whose roots are in the divisive tactics of slavery and which, by forcing men to work at great distances from their home, or to emigrate in search of a livelihood, still encourages the disruption of the family. Above the small shopkeepers and field labourers who make up the bulk of the village are the select few who have more successfully adapted to the demands of the colonial structure. These men are the most obsequious and sycophantic, acutely aware of their precarious position, balanced in the no-man's land between their 'own people' whom they despise and distrust, and the white owners and government officials to whose coat-tails they cling, and whom they seek, desperately, to imitate. Although G. is the centre of consciousness for most of the novel, Lamming steps outside these limits from time to time, presenting the viewpoint of the older generation, and commenting in a frankly authorial manner on the significance of G.'s experiences. This allows him to develop the meaning of this experience and show how it reflects the general social and political structure of colonial Barbados. Each trivial occurrence is thus linked to a pattern whose roots run back into the past (Pa and Ma) and whose consequences for the future are clearly defined. For example, the episode when one of the boys finds a letter dropped by a teacher, which contains incriminating photographs of the teacher and the headmaster's wife. The letter is a symbol of the futile little acts of rebellion with which the 'overseer' class castrate themselves, an example of the unremitting internecine warfare in which their energies are dissipated. And the reaction of the boys mirrors this process, showing its root and its blossom in a single vividly presented episode.

> The neighbour was very curious ... It was important. The neighbour had never received a letter from a girl, and he feared this boy might have been able to boast of greater success. And suppose it was the same girl. If it turned out to be the same girl they were after, what could he do? They took these things very seriously. It was their early training in the jealous response. (p. 60)

The teacher's petty act of rebellion is pointedly shown to be motivated by a desire to act out revengeful fantasies on the white world, since as well as the compromising snapshot the letter contains a pornographic photograph of 'a white couple. ... They were naked and the position was obscene'. (p. 63) Significantly, though, the revenge fantasy is perpetrated not on the white man but on one of his own kind. In this brief episode Lamming has exposed the complete psychological process and its self-destructive result. Earlier in the novel Lamming has prepared the ground for these dramatized insights by presenting their role in the society in a generalized, analytic way. Thus, what is experienced by the individual as petty frustration, irrational fear or sexual jealousy is shown to be shaped, unconsciously, by the historic forces of colonial oppression, of which the individual may remain ignorant.

> My people are low down nigger. My people don't like to see their people get on. The language of the overseer. The language of the civil servant. The myth had eaten through the consciousness like moths through the pages of ageing documents. Not taking chances with you people, my people. They always let you down ... Like children under the threat of hell-fire they accepted instinctively that the others, meaning the white, were superior ... This world of the other's imagined perfection hung like a dead weight over their energy ... you never can tell with my people. (p. 27)

As the African writer Ngugi Wa Thiong'o (James Ngugi) has said,

> In the light of what has happened to the peasant masses in Africa, the West Indies, and all over the former colonial world, *In the Castle of My Skin* acquires symbolic dimensions and new prophetic importance; it is one of the great political novels in modern 'colonial' literature.[10]

In the Castle of My Skin dramatizes through the experience of one West Indian peasant village a process which has shaped all colonized peoples. Like the African novels which deal with the rural world there is a quality of elegiac celebration in Lamming's novel. He captures a world on the point of disintegration as its inhabitants begin for the first time seriously to question the values by which it is sustained. Each stage in the process of political consciousness is represented. The novel celebrates the endurance and stoicism of the older generation, and their sense of hope for the future, expressed through their adherence to the Christian myth of salvation and a better world to come. It shows the stirrings of political and economic understanding in the 'overseer' class, and the treachery and mutual betrayal which is the inevitable product of their training and attitudes. Finally, it points to the hope for a new generation whose vision will be sharper, and whose understanding will be broadened by exposure to other societies. At the same time it is aware that this very process involves a loss and a severing of the intimacy between people and place which is the root from which the old strengths are drawn. Each of these stages is illustrated by characters who are never reduced to mere figures in a political allegory. In Lamming's vision individual lives are the stuff of history, and the understanding of the one is bound up with the other.

The culmination of the novel is G.'s departure for Trinidad, a journey of self-discovery foreshadowed in the novel by his friend Trumper's emigration to America, from which he returns imbued with a new racial consciousness. In America Trumper is made aware of his identity as a negro, and this awareness is set over against the unreal fictions that he and G. have been taught in the schools of Little England (Barbados). This awareness is linked to the experience of their people, which the colonial education system has sought to erase.

> 'I don't know much about Trinidad,' he said, regaining his composure. 'But you might got to go further one day an' there be quite a few things you got to learn. The things you got to learn in this life you never see and will never see in the books you read at that High School. 'Tis p'raps what the ol' people call experience, but take it from me, barring learning to count an' write your name there ain't much in these schools that will help you ... (p. 288)

Trumper is least surprised by the school teacher Slime's betrayal when he buys the villagers' land out from under them with their own money which he has swindled through his 'Penny Bank an' Society'. By discovering his identity, his race and its history he had discovered its accumulated wisdom. By recognizing himself as a negro he has come into his inheritance, a knowledge of betrayal, discrimination and brutality. It is an uncomfortable gain but a necessary one if there is to be any hope of change.

> 'What's the difference between us an' the black people over there?' I asked.
> ''Tis a great big difference,' said Trumper. 'They suffer in a way we don't know here. We can't understan' it here an' we never will. But their sufferin' teach them what we here won't ever know. The Race, our people.' (p. 296)

It is at this point that the boy realizes that he will one day have to leave the islands, paradoxically, to find himself. As he says,

> Trumper made his own experience, the discovery of a race, a people, seem like a revelation. It was nothing I had known, and it didn't seem I could know it till I had lived it. (p. 298)

As they finish their conversation they are startled by a crashing sound as the shoemaker's house disintegrates in a vain attempt to move it from the land out of which Slime has swindled him. Pa, the oldest man in the village, likewise cheated out of his land waits to be moved to the Alms House. As the boy prepares to make his necessary journey into exile the old world behind him is crumbling and breaking down. He is conscious that his journey is a journey in time as well as space and he reflects that he is involved in a process of loss as well as gain. He 'had seen the last of something'. (p. 303) As he goes forth to seek the identity and the inheritance which he has been denied he is aware that he and his world have changed for ever, and that in a more than simple sense there is no going back.

> The earth where I walked was a marvel of blackness and I knew in a sense more deep than simple departure I had said farewell, farewell to the land. (p. 303)

Such a departure and such an exile is, in itself, one of the great archetypes of West Indian experience. For the African the journey to Europe and America is a special and distinctive part of the social and educative process by which an élite is separated from the masses. To have 'been to', as we recall, imposes a special distinction and a certain separation on those who return. But for the West Indian, emigration in search of work, and better conditions has been a frequent and recurrent experience of all classes for many years. Thus *In the Castle of My Skin* shows three generations who have gone away from the islands in search of 'a better break'. Although economic pressure played a part it does not seem to have been the sole or even, in many cases, the primary motive. Unemployment has certainly been a problem particularly in the so-called 'small islands' after the increase of tourism and foreign land purchase has driven land prices up beyond the means of small farmers in the rural areas. But most West Indian writers seem to feel that job opportunity and better living conditions are only the rationalization of more profound and less logical urges.

To V.S. Naipaul, for instance, the urge to emigrate is the logical culmination of the inability of the West Indies to take root and form a distinctive culture. In *The Middle Passage* the emigrant ship, cruising between the islands for its passengers, is a suitable climax to a three hundred year exercise in futility and failure.

> Sometimes for as much as three months at a time a slave ship would move from anchorage to anchorage on the West African coast, picking up its cargo. The *Francisco Bobadilla* would be only five days. It would go from St. Kitts to Grenada to Trinidad to Barbados: one journey answering another: the climax and futility of the West Indian adventure.[11]

Although Naipaul castigates the attitudes of his fellow passengers towards the emigrants, and sees in it the petty, divisive snobbery which rots the fabric of West Indian society, he is not entirely free from such attitudes himself. His liberalism towards the emigrants is initially prompted by his feeling that the petty bourgeois blacks who criticize them are no better than those they criticize. But this disassociation of himself from the various groups on the ship, tourists and emigrants, is more difficult than Naipaul supposes. At first he assures himself that, like the white Portuguese crew, he and his fellow Indians are 'alien elements. Mr. Mackay and his black fellers, the tourists and the wild cows: these relationships had been fixed centuries before.' This temporary assurance of his non-involvement is shattered when he tries to approach the emigrants and is rebuffed. Their conviction that he is a 'provocateur', which he assumes the reader will reject, seems to be in part justified. His description of the motives and leaders of the group, emphasizing the lack of economic need for emigration, and the manipulation of the ignorant emigrants by educated 'leaders' would have made sweet reading to anti-immigration groups in the early sixties. Naipaul's reaction is to seek the reassurance of the only other group open to him, Mr. Mackay and the tourists who, only moments before, he has been satirizing mercilessly for their prejudiced attitude towards their fellow West Indians.

> I decided that the attitude of Mr. Mackay and Philip and Correira and most of the tourist class was healthier. They had ignored the emigrants altogether, and were in the bar. I joined them. (p. 33)

Naipaul's desperate attempt to be accepted as a special society of one, unique and above the conflict, inevitably fails. His carefully cultivated detachment breaks down in a number of places. But, more importantly, from our viewpoint, it quite prevents him from any real understanding of the emigrant, of his motives and his ideals. He is reduced to quoting newspaper paragraphs and even, at one point, to reproducing some conversation from a newspaper article in the London *Evening Standard* entitled 'I Sail With the Immigrants' though he is himself on board an emigrant ship at the time! Naipaul supposes in the passage that it is his lack of an official status which frightens off the emigrants. But one cannot help feeling that the detached, and innately superior, character of his descriptions reveals an attitude it would be difficult to hide.

> The emigrants had got out of their going-away clothes and were sitting in the sun in simpler, less constricting garments, so that the deck looked like a West Indian slum-street on a Sunday. One or two of the women had even put on slacks; the cloth was new, not yet washed, and one could detect the suitcase folds. (p. 29)

What is difficult to accept in a description like this is the feeling that the writer, for all his eye for telling detail, has failed to get inside the people he describes. They are phenomena, clinically described and categorized. The range of Naipaul's sympathetic vision does not extend to these people. As a result the passages dealing with the emigrants in *The Middle Passage* fail to engage effectively with their subject. To the reader, as to Naipaul, they remain a puzzling and impenetrable enigma.

The colonial myth, that the West Indian reality was to reflect its masters' values, and strive to imitate and emulate them is nowhere better expressed than in this continuing urge to emigrate felt by West Indians. This is an aspect of West Indian life which touches all classes of society and all races. Home, the Mother Country, the Real World, call it what you will is never here, always over there, and the call has proved irresistible to generations. The cultural pressures to leave have never been absent, but perhaps at times they have been aided and even outstripped by the economic pressures to do so. Overpopulation and unemployment is a condition of West Indian life, and a demonstrable result of nineteenth century planter policy. Indentured labourers, Indian and Chinese, continued to be imported even when the work available already outstripped the existing population. From time to time the islands have had to bleed themselves to survive. Thus emigration is an experience shared by several generations of West Indians, and a pattern etched deep into their communal memory. Thus in George Lamming's *In the Castle of My Skin* the recurring pattern is present in the old man Pa, who in his youth had emigrated to Panama to build the great canal; in the fathers of the boys who are nearly all absent (the desertion of wives preparatory to escape to Venezuela, or England is a common feature of West Indian fiction); in Trumper's emigration to America; and in the boy's recognition at the novel's end that his departure to Trinidad is only the first step in an outward bound journey from his childhood and his home.

This central and compelling pattern has been strongly marked in the writers who, like other West Indians, have from the earliest times been forced to emigrate in search of the fundamental conditions of their trade. In fact, this situation worsened in the period after the war. As Kenneth Ramchand has shown, between 1950 and 1964 the number of books published yearly in the West Indies declined substantially while the corresponding number of books written by West Indians during the same period rose. These new books were published mostly in London, and occasionally, in New York. Ramchand concludes that by the mid-sixties 'London (was) indisputably the West Indian literary capital'.[12] In more recent times young writers have consciously sought to avoid this situation. But in the period when most of the extant works were produced the act of writing and the act of emigration were inextricably bound up together.

The most sustained and effective account of the urge to leave the islands is provided by George Lamming's *The Emigrants*. The novel traces the fate of a group of emigrants travelling to England. The narrator, Collis, described as 'a writer', provides a speculative thread which holds the elements of the story together, though his reflections are occasionally intrusive and too self-conscious. The ship moves from island to island picking up its full complement of emigrants preparatory to ferrying them across the Atlantic. For some of the men and women this is the first time they have left the islands, for others it is a second voyage out, and yet all seem bound together in incomprehension as to their motives and purposes. It is as if they have been moved by forces beyond themselves, and as if on this voyage out they are as unfree and lost as their ancestors were when they were shipped out from Africa in the slave ships of the Middle Passage.

> 'This blasted world,' said Tornado, 'is a hell of a place. Why the hell a man got to leave where he born when he ain't thief not'in, nor kill nobody, an' to make it worse to go somewhere where he don't like.'[13]

Tornado and the Governor, who have been in England with

the R.A.F. during the war, are a fund of information, mostly disillusioning, about England and the reactions of the English to those coming 'Home'. But their understanding of the forces which drive them are as ill-formed as those of any of the passengers. Their disputes about the sophistication of their islands (big islands versus little islands) and the relative understanding they have of the world they sail towards is as nothing besides the general ignorance which envelopes all of them about the true reasons for this voyage they have all undertaken.

> Higgins had joined the men again. He and Tornado remained standing beside the bunks thinking on what the Governor had said. There was no big island or small island. They were leaving home with no particular desire to return, and they were sailing to a country which few had known at first hand ... He liked Trinidad. After four years in England he had had an opportunity to see whether that was true. It was. He had gone back, and now he had left again and was on his way to England. But he liked Trinidad. He was certain. (p. 44)

Collis does not overlook the immediate economic motive behind the urge to emigrate, but senses that this is only a manifestation of something deeper and more radical.

> ... every month they leave the right way, paying a passage in search of what: a better break. That's what the others say. Every man wants a better break. I've heard of others fleeing, but it seemed something quite different. Their flight was always a conscious choice, a choice even to suffer. But this isn't. This is a kind of sudden big push from the back; something that happened when you weren't looking. And now here in mid-ocean when decisions don't mean a damn because we've got no reality to test their efficacy; only here and now we realize telling ourselves with an obvious

> conviction, we want a better break. A better break. So many people wanting a better break ... (pp. 52-53)

As the characters converse they, too, speculate on their actions, and seem to feel the need to express deeper and wider motives for their journey. The urge to emigrate is seen as part of the urge of the West Indian to discover an identity, a place and a purpose. This urge is seen as manifesting itself as much in the unconscious movements and yearnings of the unskilled and semi-literate as in the conscious and educated. It is the stirrings of racial and national consciousness. In a long and vivid metaphor one of the characters compares the West Indian races to vomit spewed up by the European nations, by Africa, India and China, vomit which settled in the Caribbean. This vomit, volatile and powerful, wants to find its way back into the stomach which ejected it, but there is no stomach available. As the character concludes.

> When other people say that them is neither one thing nor the other, but just different from every other complete thing, them get frightened, sometimes shamed, till them get together an' make up their minds that them goin' prove what them is. Them all provin' something. When them stay back home in they little island them forget an' them remain vomit; just as them was vomit up, but when them go 'broad, them remember, or them get tol' w'at is w'at, an' them start to prove, an' them give w'at them provin' a name. A good name. Them is West Indians ... An' is the reason West Indies may out o' dat vomit produce a great people, 'cause them provin' that them want to be something. (pp. 67-8)

Although this process is unconscious each of the men and women on the emigrant ship is part of this movement. Their individual lives with hopes, fears and aspirations are the stuff from which history is made. As the Jamaican concludes,

> Some people say them have no hope for people who doan' know exactly w'at them want or who them is, but

> that is a lot of rass-clot talk. The interpretation me give hist'ry is people the world over searchin' an' feelin', from time immemorial ... Them ain't know w'at is wrong 'cause them ain't know w'at is right, but them keep searchin' an' feelin', an' when them dead an' gone, hist'ry write things 'bout them that them themself would not have know or understand. (p. 68)

But such an end is not to be achieved without suffering. Before any such history can come about men and women will have to live its meaningless and nameless day-to-day reality. When the boat finally arrives in England the characters are able to sustain their excitement and enthusiasm for only a short while. Their initial landing and the train journey to London confirms them in their belief that they have arrived at the heart of things, and that any difficulties can be overcome now that they are here, in this time and place.

> ... unemployment, a housing shortage. These were not important. Or were they? Starvation. Death. Yes. Even death. These were not important, for what mattered supremely was to be there, in England. (p. 106)

In the final sections of the novel the unity in fear and hope that the emigrants preserved on the boat has gradually broken down until they are reduced to isolated, suffering figures, broken and exploited, sexually and economically, by this world they have travelled so far to reach. The sordid realities of bed-sitters, of gas-fires and coffee-stalls; the world of drugs and police raids, sleazy clubs and prostitution; of rent-money and unemployment; all this is described in graphic and bitter detail. At the end of the novel the galaxy of characters is further from any self-knowledge or understanding than at the beginning, stripped now of even that hope for the future they had displayed on the voyage out. The narrator Collis has yielded his central commenting position to become just one among the figures who appear and disappear in the confused and trivial events of a daily struggle to survive. In this the novel reflects that disintegrative process which the emigrants have yielded to, and which has broken their dream of unity in the face of new experience. The final chapter presses home the point when it reintroduces the figure of the Strange Man, the character who has inspired the reveries on West Indian unity on the boat. Turning up at Governor's nightclub with a party of new arrivals for whom he is seeking accommodation he pleads for them to act on the words they had spoken earlier. Angrily, Governor discovers that his wife, whom he had deserted in the West Indies, is in the party. He throws her to the floor and the novel ends with him driving the new arrivals out of the club. The ending emphasizes the difficulties of the process of self-identity and self-assertion which the emigrants have unconsciously sought. By leaving their islands they have chosen to become part of a modern world in which identity and values are subjected to a continual, battering strain. The possibilities for self-discovery and for the forging of a new unity are not denied. But Lamming forces his characters, his readers and himself to face the full implications of the process, and its costs in human life and suffering.

A sunnier and more generous vision of the world of the emigrant is provided by the novels and short stories of Samuel Selvon. Selvon has a lighter touch than Lamming, and a sharp eye for the telling detail and the unforgettable incident. But although his treatment of the West Indian emigrant abroad is lighter and more humorous it is never frivolous or detached. Lurking in the shadows cast by this sunny humour is a thoughtful and critical observer who captures fully the ambiguity of the emigrants' feelings towards his homeland, and towards the country he has adopted.

In *The Lonely Londoners* (1956)[14] and in the London section of the short stories *Ways of Sunlight* (1957)[15] Selvon writes of the excitement and wonder of the West Indian immigrant who has arrived at the heart of that 'real world' and who, in the face of all kinds of deprivation and opposition, nevertheless clings obstinately to the magic of that dream. Moses in *The Lonely Londoners* reflects

> ... to have said: 'I walked on Waterloo Bridge', 'I rendezvoused at Charing Cross', 'Piccadilly Circus is my playground', to say these things, to have lived these things, to have lived in the great city of London, centre of the world ... What it is that would keep men although by and large, in truth, and in fact, they catching their royal to make a living, staying in a cramp-up room where you have to do everything – sleep, eat, dress, wash, cook, live. Why it is that although they grumble about it all the time ... everyone cagey about saying outright that if the chance come they will go back to them green islands in the sun? (p. 30)

He can find no answer, and seeks to reassure himself with the thought that summer will soon be here, the time when

> flowers come and now and then the old sun shining, is as if life start all over again, as if it still have time ... the summer does really be hearts.

But beneath this he is aware of the sadness and misery of existence for these men, exiled and isolated.

> He don't know the right word, but he have the right feeling in his heart. As if the boys laughing, but they only laughing because to think so much about everything would be a big calamity.

In the meantime they exist in this world as both spectators and participants, drawn to its magic like moths to a flame, and yet irresistibly reminded by the pinpricks of prejudice and antagonism that they do not quite belong,

> He lay there studying how the night before he was in the lavatory and two white fellars come in and say how these black bastards have the lavatory dirty, and they didn't know that he was there, and when he come out they say hello mate have a cigarette.

The force of Selvon's writing comes from its inside stance. He gets inside the situation of the characters and presents the world they encounter through their eyes. This unmediated presentation of the experience of the ordinary immigrant is made possible by Selvon's mastery of a natural, unstrained dialect style which exactly captures the nuances of image and thought he seeks to record. In this way Selvon is able to record the confused and ambiguous reactions of his figures.

Although these stories do not have the philosophic force of Lamming's work they are deceptively simple. Beneath the surface fragments of episode and incident Selvon has put together an image of the society the West Indian has built up for himself within an alien environment, a society with its own rules, social habits, hierarchies (based on experience of the new world), and myths. The picture he draws of this world is all the more touching and convincing because his points are never made obtrusively but emerge in action and dialogue.

The ambiguity of feeling towards England which Selvon's characters record emphasizes the force with which the educational and social myths of borrowed identity have split the West Indian from his own reality. This is not the invention of tortured intellectuals but an overwhelming and continuous pressure experienced by all classes and groups within West Indian society. It is not surprising, then, that side by side with the recording of the growth and outcome of this force the writer in the West Indies has also been concerned to explore the alternative, the acceptance of his time and place. Side by side with the novels of childhood and leavetaking we discover the novels which seek to pinpoint the here and now, the growth and characteristics of present and past realities; while the novels of emigration are matched in number only by those which deal with the experience of return. It is as if together with the urge to depart and discover there is a continuing reverse flow, the urge to return and re-discover, to define the here and now and to come to terms with what is.

Samuel Selvon's writing illustrates this double tendency.

Although he is best known, perhaps, as the chronicler of the experience of the West Indian expatriate, his most recent work has dealt strongly with the problems of life in the contemporary West Indies. *Those Who Eat the Cascadura* and *The Plains of Caroni* squarely face the problems of modern West Indian life. *The Plains of Caroni* is especially interesting because, although Selvon is still concerned primarily with the world of the East Indian rural farmer whose lifestyle formed the heart of his earlier novels set in Trinidad (*Turn Again Tiger, A Brighter Sun,* etc.) his young protagonist, Romesh, is one of those young men who have broken out of the trap of marriage and brutal hard work which captured Tiger. Romesh is steered by his ambitious mother Seeta to University and towards that 'managerial' post which represents the mecca of the canefield workers. The confusion and pain of divided loyalties which his relationship with a young white girl, Petra, and his awareness of the effects of technological change on the life of his people in the rural villages force upon him are presented with Selvon's characteristic sensitivity. Romesh and his conflicts form the core of the story but, perhaps, its main theme is the intransigence of the apathy and inertia engendered by the long years of colonialism and the difficulties involved in any attempt to change it in a meaningful way.

Selvon's concern with the problems remaining in newly independent Trinidad is tinged with the kind of disillusion which we have discussed as a quality of some recent African writing. The novel is not cynical nor despairing, but it does squarely face the fact that the attitudes bred by years of colonial dependence will not disappear overnight and will continue to militate against any effort towards change.

> Every attempt by the Government to beautify the squares and the parks of the city was doomed to failure, because there was no pride in the people. In Woodford Square, although there were asphalt pathways from every side and corner, people walked as the crow flies,

> seeking the shortest distance between two points, idle hands pulling at any young tree or decorative shrub, their feet scuffing the grass in a what-the-hell-are-you-doing-here? attitude. (p. 26-27)

The irony of this observation is, of course, increased by the fact that Woodford Square was the locale of the famous Open Air University of the first Premier of Trinidad Dr. Eric Williams. In the casual apathy of its current inhabitants there is a powerful indictment of the failure of independent politics to root out the basic malaise of this society; a failure exacerbated by the fact that the success of those who have benefited has only served to isolate them from the conditions which here persist.

> No respectable person sat to rest in Woodford Square. Indeed, there was no need to, as everyone had cars now, and the only steps they made in the city were literally those from parking-lot to office or shop. These respectable people locked themselves away in their various Fords and Chevrolets and Renaults and Vauxhalls, winding up the windows to keep out stench and noises, and they went to and from the city blind and deaf and secure, untouched and untainted. (p. 27)

Selvon's recent novels show how the attention of the West Indian writer is turning back towards the experience of life in the islands of the Caribbean as the central concern of this new literature. This tendency is also reflected in the growing number of writers who are seeking to work within their home islands; in the renewed growth of local publishing ventures; and in the development of local theatre ventures, dance companies and so forth. Attempts to deal in literature with the realities of contemporary West Indian life are not new. The next chapter seeks to trace the growth of these attempts and to illustrate some of the problems faced by those writers who have sought to express the realities of their own homelands.

SECTION 3—NOTES

1. In *Common Wealth*; ed. Anna Rutherford; Aarhus U.P.; Aarhus, 1971; p. 143.
2. ANTHONY, Michael, *Cricket in the Road and other stories*; Heinemann; Caribbean Writer's Series; London, 1973; p. 7.
3. LAMMING, George, 'The West Indian People' in *Caribbean Essays* ed. Andrew Salkey; Evans Bros.; London, 1973; p. 11.
4. LAMMING, 'The West Indian People' p. 10.
5. LAMMING, George, *In the Castle of My Skin*; Longman; London, 1970; p. 36.
6. NAIPAUL, V.S., *The Middle Passage*; Penguin; London, 1969; p. 29. First published Andre Deutsch; London, 1962.
7. ANTHONY, Michael, *Cricket in the Road*; p. 9.
8. RAMRAJ, Victor in *Common Wealth* ed. Anna Rutherford; Aarhus U.P.; Aarhus; p. 136.
9. ANTHONY, Michael, *The Year in San Fernando*; Heinemann; London, 1965.
10. NGUGI, Wa Thiong'o (James), *Homecoming*; Heinemann; London, 1972; p. 126.
11. NAIPAUL, V.S., *The Middle Passage*; p. 27.
12. RAMCHAND, Kenneth, *The West Indian Novel and its Background*; Faber; London, 1970; p. 63.
13. LAMMING, George, *The Emigrants*; Michael Joseph; London, 1954; p. 42.
14. SELVON, Samuel, *The Lonely Londoners*; Wingate; London, 1956 (reissued Longman – Caribbean, 1972).
15. SELVON, Samuel, *Ways of Sunlight*; McGibbon and Kee; London, 1957 (reissued Longman – Caribbean, 1973).

4

A SENSE OF PLACE:
Coming to Terms with the Caribbean

Colonial exploitation deprived the West Indians of the wealth of their islands and directed that wealth away in a stream of overseas investment which makes small beer of the booty hauled off by buccaneers and Spanish conquistadores. But, more importantly, as we have seen, its side effects deprived him of the possession of the islands in a spiritual sense. This lost sense of place and identity has been something against which generations of West Indians have struggled. The most widespread alienation stems, of course, from the dispossession of the negro and his forcible 'planting' in a strange, isolated landscape. But the other West Indian racial groups have experienced a similar, if less radical, dislocation. Thus the indentured labourers, Indian or Chinese, brought in to supplement slave-labour in the nineteenth century were also dispossessed, though they struggled to maintain the social patterns of their original cultures. Unfortunately, these remnants of an inherited culture often only served to prevent the development of even a rudimentary sense of identification with their new homelands. The creole white population, although nominally 'in control' of their surroundings, were also desperately ill at ease in the islands from which they drew their wealth. Frantically imitative of the 'home' culture they were resolute in denying anything but a proprietary identification with the islands they exploited so ruthlessly.

For each of the many racial groups which make up the West Indian population the ideal with which they identified lay outside the reality of their experience. For the black West Indian, as we have seen, the educational pattern insisted that all values were the prerogative of England and that the path of advancement lay in an imitation of these values. For the descendant of the Indian indentured labourer the only alternative was to remain isolated within a culture radically disrupted by the new geographical location and the interdependence of racial groupings in economic and social terms: how could Hinduism remain an effective source of values in a land where all castes of men were effectively enslaved? Or where the young Brahmin setting out on his pilgrimage to sacred Benares had to halt when he reached the sea at Port o' Spain?

These inherent difficulties have led the West Indian writer into a conscious struggle to discover a form which will enable West Indians to see themselves and each other. As we saw in the last chapter, many West Indian writers have turned to the world of the child to discover new structures which reproduce the experience of this new world. Others have approached the problem in a more historical way, seeking to record the growth of the new self-consciousness which led to the struggle for independence and self-definition. In the West Indies, as in Africa, the literary work and the political struggle were often closely related. N.W. Manley, the former Jamaican premier, has described this relationship.

> The new birth in Jamaica in 1938 did many things, but one thing stands out like a bright light ... Our best young men plunged deep into the lives of the people and came up with poems and paintings and with vivid and powerful books ... It was a strange world they discovered; strange, most of all, in the fact that it was not a

world where different cultures had blended into any single significant pattern, but a world divided and split in a manner as peculiar as it was deep-seated. It was not just a question of colour, nor yet of rich and poor; it was a matter of differences that involved widely different acceptances and rejections of values, different interpretations of reality, the use of identical words to express different concepts and understandings.

No Jamaican writer working in those early days of our National Movement could do a greater service for us all than to interpret that other world to which the majority belong for the rest of us to see and understand.[1]

Apart from the unconscious élitism of the last sentence, this statement is an effective and clear definition of the task to which many West Indian writers addressed themselves in the period immediately after the Second World War. For many the approach was historical. They were acutely conscious that the history of the West Indies had deprived its inhabitants of a 'single significant pattern' of thought and feeling; yet they were aware too that even in the divided society of Jamaica or Trinidad new forces were stirring. These forces had their roots in the history of humiliation and deprivation which all West Indians shared. Through an investigation of this history a beginning could be made in the exploration of the common ties binding this multiplicity of peoples together, ties forged largely from disappointment and failure, but no less powerful and meaningful for that, and the clear source of inspiration for the new demands for political independence. It is this examination of the continuities of Jamaican history which underlies Vic Reid's *New Day* (1949), an examination which made it such an important and influential work. Many critics have stressed the importance of Reid's novel as one of the earliest statements of the discovery of a West Indian consciousness. Gerald Moore has called it the first announcement of the discovery of the West Indian 'that (he) is neither a rootless being devoid of identity, nor a lost son of Africa or

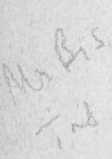

Asia, but a man made and shaped by this island now'.[2] As he says,

> This novel rests upon a single proposition, that Jamaica has a history. This history is distinct from its various racial groups separately viewed ... It follows that there is such a creature as a Jamaican, and that we can only get to know him by looking at his island and following his story.[3]

Mervyn Morris, in his introduction to the long-overdue reissue of the novel, describes *New Day* as 'a dialect work with a sense of national mission', part and parcel of 'a period of national awakening in the arts as in politics'.[4] While Louis James opens his essay on Reid with the comment that

> V.S. Reid's *New Day* ... was a pioneering claim that a West Indian island could have its own national history and culture. By focusing on the life of the common people and on their popular idiom ... Reid foreshadowed important elements in the literary movements that were to follow.[5]

Reid makes his point by focusing his treatment of West Indian history through one figure. The aged Johnny Campbell, at the end of his life, on the eve of the 1944 Independence celebrations at which his grandson is to accept the leadership of his people reflects on his experience. His life spans the period between the futile and desperate Morant Bay Rebellion of 1865 and the success of the National Movement for Jamaican self-government. The story of Johnny Campbell can be used to structure a history of the Jamaican people and to chronicle the growth of their own consciousness of themselves as unique and meaningful. In addition the novel is the first to employ a modified form of creole dialect not only for dialogue but also for narration. Its very form celebrates the new possibilities inherent in the Jamaican heritage it chronicles. Furthermore, the use of modified dialect stresses the novel's aim to present the

Jamaican experience from inside, and so demonstrates Reid's belief in the inherent interest and meaningfulness of the life of the ordinary Jamaican, past and present. Johnny Campbell is a member of the light-skinned 'buckra' plantermen family whose ancestors led the rebellion and whose descendants lead the struggle for self-determination. Johnny Campbell's lifetime begins at the time when these natural leaders, who occupy a privileged position as 'overseers', are gradually realizing that their interests are the same as those of the mass of the Jamaican people.

> 'Now, then, Johnny, you know how our parish people like to tell howdy to one another. If the two of us pass them and do not say howdy, you know what they will say?' Tongue-tied me, and just a-listen for what parish people will say if we no' tell them howdy.
>
> 'They will say we are playing like *buckra*,' says Davie. Is not bad, that? Then why Davie serious so? I am a-think that *buckra* are great people; for ride, they ride horses all the time and do not walk like negroes and poor whites.
>
> Then why Davie serious so?
>
> 'And Mas'r-No'-Tell-Howdy-Johnny, the day is a-come soon when all *buckra* plantermen will be sorry they ha-passed and not tell howdy-ho!'[6]

As Johnny's story unfolds we follow the development of this natural group of leaders within the society, and the lesson they learn through defeat and bloodshed that the road to success is by political organization not futile military rebellion. At the end of the novel there is a celebratory note as Garth Campbell, descendant of that Davie who led the rebellion outlines the future to the people.

> ... from Westmoreland parish to St. Thomas-in-the East, Garth is telling everybody that they must follow who they will, but not to cease a-holler for the new constitution. From Westmoreland parish to St. Thomas, from Trelawney parish to the bottom lands o'Vere, men

hear the voice o' Davie's seed talking without fear in his throat ...

Hear my boy a-thunder in the finish of his race! No turnings now for him. He is marching along the road what his grand spoke of to the Queen's Commissioners ... Many leaders ha' gone into his blood. My boy is a-thunder in the finish o' his race, and man has no' been made yet that can stop him. (pp. 337-8)

New Day ends on a note of hope for possibilities ahead. The new Constitution offers a future radically different from any available in the past; different, Reid implies, because it is the visible expression of the new spirit of unity forged in the political and social struggle for Independence. As Garth says,

... in our island we have proven that race is but skin-shallow and that we are brothers in the depth of us – give us liberty to walk as Jamaicans ... (p. 338)

Perhaps Reid's optimism in 1949 has been less than justified by subsequent events, but the goal he defines has been one for which West Indians have striven consciously ever since, and the literature which follows reflects the struggle's successes and failures.

Hand in hand with the struggle for historical definition went the struggle to direct attention to the actual conditions which shaped West Indian lives. The earliest, and still one of the most potent, writers who addressed themselves to this task was the Jamaican, Roger Mais. In the period between the war and his death in 1955 he produced three powerful studies of Jamaican life and left unfinished a fourth work on an even larger scale.[7] In Roger Mais's novels Jamaican life and Jamaican people are treated with a passionate sense of their intrinsic interest and value. Mais piles detail on detail to create with absolute fidelity the reality of the experience he records. Here, for example, in a typical passage, we are taken inside the experience through the vivid, concrete detail. This world is realized, not simply clinically 'described' from some superior, outside vantage point.

Goodie thought it was Puss-Jook but it was Ditty wheezing a little bronchially in her untroubled sleep on a mattress laid out on the floor one corner of the room. Puss-Jook was doing no more than scratching himself systematically and with the greatest economy of effort over by the window staring out into the night when she came back from Cousin Maudie's down the road with the liniment for her knee. Took up cold in it she had from standing long in her rubber-sole canvas shoes on the chill pavement outside the grassyard early mornings haggling over vegetables she bought from the country people coming in on trucks from the hills.

She had run out of liniment, careless, but really sake of she didn't have time before doctor shop closing to buy it bring home with her. Night fall so soon, you take two turns round the market square with your vegetable barrow, tired, siddung, shet you' eye, open it, Lawd, sun gone down.[8]

Mais's prose as can be seen in this extract, reflects the rhythms of dialect speech without attempting a full scale literary approximation in the manner of Reid. This provides him with a greater flexibility, and allows him to avoid the monotony of Reid's rhythms. But he retains the inside stance, his prose seeming to follow the development of his characters' thoughts rather than just reproducing them. Mais's technical achievement in his novels seems to me to have been underrated by most critics who have ignored or criticized his style and concentrated on his passion and social anger. Although he has been justly criticized for lapses into sentimentality and prolixity[9]

(Tears came to her eyes, and they were not all for smoke, ... a dark mist came up inside her and her bosom grew big with her troubles and the burden of her days and nights).[10]

the accuracy and directness of his descriptive writing has

rarely been matched in the West Indian novel to date. But the heart of Mais's achievement is not technical. What he did was to present a view of Jamaican life from inside, an uncompromising and complete picture of the suffering and misery of day to day existence in the Kingston slums. His novels celebrate the strength and spirit of the Jamaicans who inhabit these slums, and shows the impoverished existence of those who, ironically, ought to be heirs to the most beautiful island in the West Indies. In this Jamaica there are no tourist pictures of gleaming beaches and blue, forest-clad mountains. These novels reflect a world whose unremitting demands shut out everything but the immediate daily grind. Poverty, crime and dirt are ever-present realities; race and colour the sources of conflict and petty snobbery; while sexual passions alternatively assauge and irritate his characters' restricted feelings. In his first novel, *The Hills Were All Joyful Together*, Mais details the lives of the inhabitants of a Jamaican yard. In a manner reminiscent of the tenement plays of Sean O'Casey he abjures narrative and plot in favour of a fragmentary, imagistic series of scenes in which each character is introduced as an aspect of the life of the yard. In a sense the yard itself is the subject of the novel, a setting which so permeates and governs the actions of its inhabitants that their lives are inseparable from the conditions it imposes on them. Gradually a series of patterns emerge defining conditions which are the springs of individual lives. Zephyr, the warm-hearted whore; Euphemia, the seductive wife of Shag who awakens to sexuality through an unwanted but irresistable physical passion for the no-good Bajun Man; Shag himself, a dying man, whose pent-up violence is released viciously and pointlessly by circumstances which he can barely comprehend; all these and others interact in a story whose motivation is in the physical and economic conditions they must all endure. Out of the pattern several main strands emerge. First, the tension between Euphemia and Shag, which culminates in the bloody murder of Euphemia when Shag runs amok with his matchet. Throughout this story, the overwhelming impression is of the helplessness of both characters; Euphemia's inability to resist the physical passion which alone seems to provide a meaning to life in the yards is matched by Shag's inability to stifle the violence which alone can cut through the tangle of despair and deprivation in which all are trapped. After he has committed the murder in which he literally hacks Euphemia to pieces he dies, broken and futile, no closer to realization or to fulfilment ...

> Women all around him went on weeping, wringing their hands, talking, making strange noises.
> He felt this weakness overcome him. He put his head down between his knees and brought up great gouts of blood.
> He was dying, he knew it, this was his death warrant signed on the flagstones between his feet, in blood. And he couldn't care less.[11]

Counterpointing this is the story of Surjue and his wife Rema. Surjue as the character list states is, 'impatient and wants to get on.' But his ambition only leads him to a life of petty crime, and finally to prison. The bitterness of her fate drives Rema to despair and to the refuge of madness. The brutality of life in the prison, and the desire to see Rema, news of whose illness has reached him, drives Surjue into a desperate attempt to escape. Inevitably this ends in failure, and Surjue is shot while attempting to scale the wall of the prison. Ironically, Rema has died in a fire started by herself before the escape attempt is made.

Zephyr's survival is due, perhaps, to her acceptance of the crushing limits of life in the yard. Her refusal to become emotionally involved with the persistent Lennie is, perhaps, a subconscious recognition that in this world only those with minimal and transitory passions can hope to get by. Only Lennie escapes, with his decision to go to America, where like Trumper in Lamming's *In the Castle of My Skin*, he will no doubt find new agonies, new ghettoes, and, perhaps, new hopes.

The younger generation of the yard, Manny, Wilfie, Tansy and the others act out the passions and despairs of their elders in miniature. Nothing better seems to be prepared for them by fate than to re-enact the drudgery and violence of their parents.

All the action of the novel is viewed in tight close-up, and perspective is deliberately restricted. There is very little description emphasizing the restriction imposed by enclosing shanty walls, the closed in yard, the bottle-strewn gullies and the enclosed spaces of prison and hospital. Only at the very end of the novel is there some hint of a wider horizon of possibility, but one which ironically is only approachable through death. As Surjue is shot we switch rapidly from the intensely restricted world of his impressions to the outer world which he has tried literally and metaphorically to reach but from which conditions have effectively barred him. For an instant that is too small to count or reckon he must have felt the steel-jacketed bullet tearing through his flesh, just under his right shoulder blade.

> And that was all. Darkness of the night eternal and absolute shut upon him. He hung suspended another instant, and then he seemed to let go all he had won so desperately ... fell back with a thud to the ground below. He fell spread-eagled on his back, and lay still. A scudding, shapeless mass of filmy clouds drew over the face of the moon. The stars put out again. A dog howled in the darkness outside the wall.
>
> He lay on his back, his arms flung wide, staring up at the silent unequivocal stars.[12]

In this and in the novels which follow Mais presents one of the earliest and strongest condemnations of colonial policies in contemporary West Indian life. Beyond the edges of the action hovers a human system which enforces the conditions under which the characters suffer, though they themselves are never able fully to see the pressures which cause their slums to exist and flourish. Thus Surjue's death is, in part, provoked by the narrowness and viciousness of the prison system with which white, colonial society seeks to contain the violence of the slums created by their own economic priorities. Trapped within the system the black Jamaican is powerless to perceive, let alone alter, the conditions which pervert and destroy his human potential. V.S. Naipaul has commented on the absence of a tradition of protest writing in the West Indies comparable with that produced by Black Americans. While this has been largely true, the novels of Roger Mais show that from early on the West Indian writer has had the potential to depict the viciousness, and narrowness of the system fostered on him by his masters, and squarely to face the crippling consequences of this life for the West Indian peoples.

That such pioneer work did not lead to a tradition of politically conscious protest writing is due to a number of factors. Not least among these was the escape route provided by emigration, both to the Mother Country which continued to be represented to the West Indian as 'home' in schools and in popular myth, and to America. The potential protest leaders of the West Indies are synonymous with the revolutionary leaders of movements in America, and in Africa (Claude McKay, Marcus Garvey and George Padmore, for example). The notable exception has been in the semi-political, popular religious movements, such as the Ras Tafarian movement in Jamaica and elsewhere. In fact, until recently, religious sects of varying political colour seem to have absorbed most of the force of protest in the West Indies and to have provided the source of consolation and expression for the pent-up feelings bred by poverty and discrimination. Roger Mais' second novel *Brother Man* shows the tragedy of just such a religious/political prophet. Struggling desperately to find some source of consolation to ease the pain of a life steeped in poverty and misery Bra' Man turns to the philosophy of resignation and love.

> He spoke in simple, down-to-earth language

telling them that they were to turn away from evil and to follow after righteousness. And many, realizing that was all he had to say, turned away in disappointment, and some turned aside to mock, but even when they had gone there was still a great crowd left who listened to him ...[13]

But in itself this philosophy is insufficient to do more than allay the symptoms of the disease of deprivation which assails the crowd, and like his Master before him the new prophet of love is torn down by those who worshipped him. The violence and sexual crime which is a constant companion to their poverty and distress demands scapegoats, and the religious prophets of the Ras Tafarian sect are blamed for a murder and rape committed by 'a bearded man'. Bra' Man is identified in the eyes of the crowds with the sect, though he is not in fact a Ras Tafarian. But it is enough for the crowd that an excuse exists to allow them to vent their disappointment and rage that the consolations of religion have not altered their lives. Only in the sweet passion of violence can they find a momentary satisfaction, some tangible object of hate on which to vent their pent up frustration and disillusionment.[14]

> When they had mauled him to the satisfaction of their lust, they voided on him and fouled him. A woman showed them how.
> The crowd rocked and screamed and crowed with laughter. Others suddenly realized that they too wanted to make water ... and then, as it happens, the game went stale. It suddenly lost its zest.
> They shifted uneasily on their feet. One by one they slunk away.
> They went to their several homes, threading their way through the narrow, squalid lane. A silence had fallen upon them, and the fears and frustrations, which were the constant companions of their thoughts, came home to roost again.[15]

A broad and objective examination of the conditions of West Indian life by writers has been made more difficult by the racial complexity of this culture. The many racial and religious divisions have often prevented the West Indian from attaining a sense of his own unique identity, offering him instead a temporary consolation and refuge in exclusiveness. For many West Indians their lives are lived within such an exclusiveness, a world within a world. The problem of such groups, and the question of their ability to survive has grown more acute in recent years as increased urbanization, education and travel have splintered their unity. A process of gradual creolization has set in. Viewed from outside this process may be welcomed as a step forward towards a wider regional identity; but from within the process may seem as much a loss as a gain. This reaction has been most notable amongst Indian-descended West Indians, who have sometimes viewed creolization as an euphemism for domination by those of negro descent. The example of British Guiana and its recent history of divisive racial politics stands as a warning of what can occur. Comparing the reactions of two Indian descended Trinidadian writers, V.S. Naipaul and Sam Selvon, to creolization Gerald Moore has emphasized the inevitability of the process and the fruitlessness of writers wishing it away, or ignoring it. Using Selvon's characters Tiger and Urmila from *A Brighter Sun* as examples of the new style Indians, integrated with their black neighbours, and reflecting their creolization in life-style and speech-pattern, he comments

> Naipaul does not seem to recognize that people like these will soon need to define a West Indian existence, call it nationalism or what you will, quite as urgently as their Creole compatriots.[16]

Significantly, considering his stand, Naipaul has never dealt seriously with these figures. In his early work like *Miguel Street, The Suffrage of Elvira* and *The Mystic Masseur* the interaction of Indian and negro, of Chinese and mulatto is implicit, but despite his unsurpassed eye for recording detail and his ready compassion for their suffering and deprivation Naipaul's view of the relations between these inhabitants of the urban slum and straggling rural village is dominated by his sense of their shared eccentricity and pathos. For Naipaul they are united beyond their racial differences in their shared lack of serious meaning. There is no sense here, as in Selvon's novels, of a new kind of man emerging, uniquely and distinctly West Indian. This reflects the general tone of Naipaul in these early novels and short stories. Even in the superb depiction of the confidence trickster-cum-pundit Ganesh, the hero of *The Mystic Masseur*, the effect is undercut by the feeling that Naipaul does not believe that any aspect of Ganesh's career really merits serious concern. The bitter comedy of the final meeting between the narrator and the resplendent G. Ramsay Muir M.B.E. on an English railway station is only incidentally satiric and is allowed to shade off into a fitting climax to a comedy of postures in which the overriding emotion is disdain and a gentle, superior humour. These limitations in Naipaul's vision can be seen more clearly, perhaps, if we compare the presentation of Ganesh with that of Achebe's Chief Nanga in *A Man of the People*. Although Achebe is equally sure-footed in pointing up the comic pretentiousness in Nanga's behaviour and the ironic implication of his position as Minister of Culture he never for a moment loses sight of the serious political and social implications of this in the Nigerian context. For Achebe, unlike Naipaul, the world he is writing about is an important one; for Naipaul, as he has indicated, the West Indian experience remains a comic sideshow, the main event being staged elsewhere. Interestingly, much of this attitude spills over into Naipaul's treatment of modern Africa in his recent novella *In a Free State*. For Naipaul the tragedy of colonialism lies in the fact that it leaves behind it either a vacuum or a pretentious, imitative fiction of itself. Naturally, this condition is heightened where, as in the West Indies, there are few pre-colonial patterns on which to fall back; or where the alternative patterns (e.g. Indian) are imported and subject to decay. He seems to reject completely the possibility of effective new patterns establishing themselves.

Such a make-believe world can only maintain its structures by a series of elaborate pretences, and from this fictional and futile existence the only effective escape is in death or flight. Naipaul explores this thesis most effectively when he applies it to the world of the Indian sub-culture in which he grew up. At the time this still retained a high degree of cohesion and exclusivity centring on religious and social custom. Yet this cohesiveness is seen as intrinsically unstable, and always potentially comic, since it can only be maintained by a series of half-hearted compromises and partial truths. Although such a world provides a refuge and a source of consolation it only does so for those prepared to turn a blind eye to its inherent contradictions and falsities. In *A House for Mr. Biswas* Naipaul explores the tensions of an individual trapped in such a society through a series of powerful and evocative metaphors. Biswas's fate defines the limits of possibility Naipaul sees in the West Indian situation, its positive and its negative extremities. After this for him and for his characters there is nothing left but flight and denial.

Mohun Biswas, the novel's hero, is a Trinidadian Indian whose sole advantage lies in his Brahmin status. Marked out for misfortune from his birth by omen and circumstance we begin to sense in him a figure who, in accordance with Naipaul's general ideas, is indeed unfortunate in his time and place. His childhood unfolds as a series of daydreams, punctuated by sores, illnesses and occasional brief moments of glory when his Brahmin status makes him desirable to flesh out a ceremony or ritual; moments which only serve to underline the unreal nature of caste and custom in this society. Throughout the story of his childhood the omniscient narrator often jumps forward to episodes not yet related, or makes comparisons with later occasions in Biswas's life which the reader has not yet encountered, as if to stress the limitations inherent in the hero's situation from the beginning.

Referring to one of the ceremonial occasions at which Mr. Biswas's Brahminical presence is required the narrator comments,

> ... as soon as the ceremony was over and he had taken his gift of money and cloth and left, he became once more only a labourer's son ... And throughout life his position was like that. As one of the Tulsi sons-in-law and as a journalist he found himself among people with money ... but always, at the end, he returned to his crowded, shabby room.[17]

Ambitious in an undirected way, Mr. Biswas, as he is referred to throughout, takes up sign-painting. A job at Hanuman House, the store-cum-tribal-home of the Tulsi family leads him into the clutches of Old Mrs. Tulsi (Mai), a widow, overblessed with daughters, whom she marries off with little care except for the proprieties of Hindu caste law. The sons-in-law she acquires in this way provide the overseers and workforce for the family. Mr. Biswas's Brahmin status meeting the Tulsi needs he is quickly bullied into marriage with one of the daughters and joins the Tulsi circus. Mr. Biswas is immediately aware in an undefined way that by becoming part of the Tulsi household he has sacrificed his liberty and his future and yet he is also seduced by the security and certainty which this surrender brings as reward. He solves his problem by accepting the latter, and kicking against the pricks by a hundred and one small acts of defiance and disrespect which quickly brings him the name of troublemaker and disturber of the peace. The great rambling Tulsi household, ill-defined and yet curiously hierarchical; eclectic in religious practice, yet noisily pious; generous within limits, yet unrelenting in its demands, is a single, comprehensive, brilliantly evoked metaphor for the traditional Indian community. Against this world Biswas struggles to maintain an independence, swinging between anger at its blandishment and emotional blackmail, and self-recrimination against his own ingratitude and obvious inability to survive alone. Against the traditional, static Tulsi values Biswas hurls a stream of revolutionary ideas: economic independence; caste reform; self-help; and love-marriage. Throughout his life he tries to escape the Tulsi embrace, as a field overseer, and later, as a hack-journalist and a social welfare worker. But, although he manages to establish areas of independence he can never completely break away from the household, and must submit to his wife and children remaining tied to the Tulsi ménage, a condition he can only view obscurely as a form of betrayal. In this struggle the idea of a house of his own becomes an obsession, a symbol of an independence that always eludes him. Yet Biswas's struggle against the Tulsi values is never complete. He is always, despite himself, seduced into a resentful admiration of its vigour and warmth. Soon that world begins to disintegrate. The sons of Mrs. Tulsi, the household gods of the establishment, are alienated by education and travel, and Seth, the economic lynch-pin, is driven from the household. Mr. Biswas's reaction is a mixture of satisfaction and fear. Although he has scorned the Tulsi values he has always depended on them as a reassuring reality against which he can oppose his own schemes and daydreams, and to which he can always return, chastened if undefeated, when they fail to work out. Now that reality is fading there is nothing effective he can visualize to take its place. The break-up of the Tulsi world is not presented in isolation. It is shown as part of the general and widespread changes in the island brought about by war. The American soldiers and their bases bring a new, fluid economic atmosphere to the islands and a social mobility not dependent on race, caste or family patronage. Ironically, this is the world Mr. Biswas has advocated; the independent, self-reliant ideal he nourishes in his crowded room as he thumbs through his copies of Samuel Smiles and Marcus Aurelius, his talismans against the Tulsi world. But when it arrives Mr. Biswas is unable to accommodate it, or it him.

In daylight, in a *Sentinel* motorcar and with a *Sentinel* photographer, he drove through the open plain to call on Indian farmers to get material for his feature on Prospects For This Year's Rice Crop. They, illiterate, not knowing to what he would return that evening, treated him as an incredibly superior being. And these same men who, like his brothers, had started on the estates and saved and bought land of their own, were building mansions; they were sending their sons to America and Canada to become doctors and dentists. There was money in the island ... And from this money, despite Marcus Aurelius and Epictetus, despite Samuel Smiles, Mr. Biswas found himself barred. (p. 438)

Mr. Biswas remains tied to the Tulsi world because, despite his wishes, he remains a sideshoot of those values, aberrant but still rooted in the same stock. In a way he is a representative figure of a generation caught between the security of the old world and the possibilities of the new, a man trapped in the transitional phase between two worlds. But he is also more than that. Naipaul has invested the figure of Biswas with a symbolic force which overspills social and historical bounds. In a hundred tiny strokes he builds Biswas into a figure whose dreams embody those of all men struggling to define an identity and to resist conformity to social habit and custom. Biswas is man as artist (his sign-painting, his abortive short stories), as religious reformer (his theological brushes with Hari), as social rebel (his brushes with authority in all forms), and, perhaps pre-eminently, as jester. Above all Biswas is comic. His man-child precociousness; his awful practical jokes; his lugubrious and wordy humour, have the comic pathos we associate with the great, traditional clowns, inept and yet wise thorns in the world's side. In Biswas Naipaul has succeeded in balancing his compassion for the West Indian people and his sense of the grotesque, farcical comedy of their condition and has created a figure in which comic ineptitude is a badge of humanity not a sign of cultural primitiveness. Biswas's failings are presented as the failings of man in all times and places, his problems and his dreams as common to all humanity, and not as in Naipaul's earlier work as the special grotesque marks which characterize the West Indian. Thus Biswas can answer his son Anand's query 'Who are you?' with the unconscious wisdom of the human clown in all ages: 'I am just somebody. Nobody at all. I am just a man you know.' (p. 279) And like man he recognizes that his limitation is his strength and that within these limitations his own creativity and imagination is a force which mirrors the creative force of God himself. As Biswas's life unfolds we recognize that his dreams and his weakness, his hopes and his failures are an effective chart of the stretches and limits of the human imagination.

> He showed Anand how to mix colours. He taught him that red and yellow made orange, blue and yellow green.
> 'Oh. That is why the leaves turn yellow?'
> 'Not exactly.'
> 'Well, look then. Suppose I take a leaf and wash it and wash it and wash it, it will turn yellow or blue?'
> 'Not really. The leaf is God's work. You see?'
> 'No.'
> 'Your trouble is that you don't really believe. There was a man like you one time. He wanted to mock a man like me. So one day, when the man like me was sleeping, this other man drop an orange in his lap, thinking, "I bet the damn fool going to wake up and say that God drop the orange." So the other man woke up and began eating the orange. And this man come up and say, "I suppose God give you that orange." "Yes," the other man said. "Well, let me tell you. Is not God. Is me." "Well," the other man said, "I prayed for an orange while I was asleep."' (p. 280)

Biswas does not revolt against established customs because of social or political beliefs, which is why he can no more accommodate the new values than the old. His revolt is against any value system which denies the intrinsic importance of man and the autonomous power of the individual to renew the experience of the race through the experience of his own life. What Biswas stands for is the human right to fail in one's own unique way and because of this although at the end of his life he dies in possession of only a caricature of his dream of responsibility and freedom; a house, shamelessly and cunningly jerry-built, foisted on him by deception, the reader remains deeply aware of the heroism and importance of his struggle and what it represents. In *A House for Mr. Biswas* Naipaul has found in the West Indian reality the material for a unique and powerful statement about the human condition. It is, perhaps, the tragedy of this troubled and brilliant writer that he has been unable to accept what he has discovered.

The present seems to force itself into West Indian fiction only with great reluctance. An unqualified present, that is, and not one aided by a special viewpoint, or by a reassuring geographical distance. The writer who is able to come to terms with the special conditions of his childhood seems more reluctant to face the situation of the adult West Indian in the here and now. Just as Jamaica provided the first real attempt at recording the growth of an historical consciousness, and the first serious studies of the life of the contemporary ghetto, so it is Jamaican writers who have tried to write of the new groups of young men and women who, benefiting from the constitutional struggle of the forties, form the new salaried élite. John Hearne, though often dismissed by critics as a writer obsessed with the trappings of the good life, and overdependent on the American-style novel of sex and social issues has, nonetheless, provided a series of studies of the Jamaican middle-class which serve to remind us that a society has emerged from the slave-history of the West Indies whose taboos, excitements, political allegiances and class-prejudices are as complex and difficult to define as those of the societies with which they are inextricably bound up. But it is the work of another Jamaican-bred writer, Andrew Salkey, which I want to consider in this context. Salkey's novel *The Late Emancipation of Jerry Stoker* is unusual in its conscious attempt to deal with the experience of being educated, middle-class and salaried in a society where poverty and deprivation remain the norms. The novel is unusual too, in its clear awareness of how it relates to the pioneer attempts to come to terms with Jamaican realities. The very first sentence places the novel not only in Jamaican history but in its relation to the hopes of the early pioneers of Jamaican literature such as Reid.

It was a long time after the New Constitution of 1944.

It was the time of public anguish for parents whose sons and daughters were not selected by the Civil Service Appointments' Board ... It was also the time of the coming élite of the Ministries.[18]

In the story which follows, which traces the struggle of just such a young élitist to see and come to terms with the world he lives in, Salkey unerringly defines the gap between the expectations of Reid's generation and the realities of his own. But he does so without bitterness, and with a compassion for the confused, well-meaning young men and women who have to live in it. As he says at the end of the Prologue, for those who lived it, 'It was a halcyon time', even though it was 'a splendid time for the desk, and a rotten time for the land.'

Adolescence and early manhood is not an easy period to write about whether the subject is a person or a society. The enthusiasms, forced cynicism, even the sacrifices of the young have an inevitable self-consciousness which it is difficult for a writer to convey forcefully without himself becoming suspect. Salkey's novel does not escape this flaw fully. But in compensation we get a detailed and valuable inside picture of the deadness of the new society for those who are trapped in it, a deadness brought about not by lack of intelligence or will-power, but by the overwhelming sense that the issues which face them are painted dummies see-sawing inanely above a sea of apathy, indifference, and cynical outside manipulation.

> It was the time of the Kirby-Rybic Kingdom, the unique duo of opposing politicians who opposed each other's theories but served common Whitehall ends. (p. 2)

From the beginning there is a sense of inevitability in the outcome, a sense reinforced by the simple but effective device of contrasting the rebellious, roustabout reaction of Jerry with that of his resigned but equally thwarted brother, Les.

> Jerry knew that many of Les's plans had been frustrated but he was unable to make the first move to sympathise or even to talk things over with him. Les, in turn, was also aware of Jerry's attempts to escape the Island's extreme colonial stranglehold, but he, too, was unable to make the first move to show his understanding of the situation. Yet there were certain secret concessions which they granted each other. Jerry's devotion to revolt and escape and his efforts to encourage his friends to break out of their prolonged depression made Les think of his brother with respect and admiration. Jerry respected Les's love of music and Les's ability to live with his unrealised dream and carry on in spite of his blighted future. (p. 14)

The crowd of young civil servants, journalists, and immigrant Europeans with whom Jerry seeks consolation, and whom he strives to stir from their rum-soaked apathy seem at first to him to be a potential source of change, an alternative to the see-sawing of politicians and the continual snobberies of colour and race.

> ... While Jerry, Silba, Albert and Paula were discussing the doubtful merits of the Kirby-Rybik Kingdom, NEXUS, Prudence Kirby's literary review, and class and caste in the Island, it occurred to Jerry that all they were really doing was trying to bore away at the *status quo* over cheap rum and water, and he said so quite strongly.
>
> 'If that's the case,' Paula suggested, 'why not let's

think of ourselves as termites, threatening the system in the afternoon?'

'Right,' Albert said. 'We're Termites from now on, *to rass!*' (p. 26)

But, as the narrative makes clear, the Termites are themselves riddled with the same prejudices and limitations; self-consciously aware of colour and class; and as dependent as anyone else in their world on the benevolence of government salary-cheques and the consolation of meaningless ritual.

The Termites always sat at two round tables, in the same position and in the same order, on Civil Service pay days. (p. 29)

The portion of the novel which deals with Jerry's involvement with the Termites is, perhaps, too long, and occasionally repetitive as one description of a drinking bout merges with the next. But as a study of the floating world of Kingston and the imperceptible way its delights shade off and cross the barriers of class and race, providing a welcome, if superficial, escape from the problems the new West Indian élite faces, it has its purpose and its point. Gradually Jerry begins the slow rejection of this temporary solution weaning himself off the continual Black Seal rum 'pitches' and seeking alternative consolations, first in a love affair, and finally, in a relationship with a Rastafarian brother whom he meets, a resident of the Dung'll, a shanty town refuge for derelicts and outcasts. At first his intention is to live on the Dung'll with Bashra, the Rastafarian, and teach, to provide the illiterates with the education denied them by their society, But he is quickly involved in the realization that the only possible solution to the problems posed are political. Early in the novel Jerry has envisaged the Rastafarian brotherhood as an alternative political force to the Kirby-Rybik Kingdom (p. 18). He is less concerned with its religious rhetoric and its proposed return to a mythic Ethiopia than with the possibility that it may be the core for a party aimed at the politicization of the

Kingston slum inhabitants, ignored by the racially orientated major parties. As the story progresses a gap is exposed between the intentions of Jerry and those whom he seeks to mould.

Jerry's first attempt to draw the Brothers into direct action is a fiasco, exposing not only their differences with him but also the splits within the Brotherhood's own ranks.

The march which Jerry and his friends help to organize succumbs to the universal apathy of the society

> ... nothing happened. There was no reaction from the small groups of undergraduates who looked on passively, innocently. No reaction from the Mona villagers. None from the University staff in their houses on College Common. (pp. 204-5)

The march serves only to emphasize the misconception Jerry and his helpers have of the manner in which the Rastafarians are shaping. To the militant element, the so-called Blood and Thunder Brethren, his March is an example of the naive system-acceptance which for them characterizes the middle-class he is struggling to reject. As their leader tells Bashra when they refuse to join the marchers

> ... You like peace an' love; we buil' with blood an' t'under. You 'ave outside people, like these two nice middle-class boys an' the others, 'elpin' you out; we got *we* alone. You' extendin' the Brethren too far 'mongst the wrong element; we' militant an' tough an' tight bad ... we goin' take over from you, Bashra, an' be the big force you was. We goin' put you out to pasture an' grab all the Rasta an' organize them. Wait an' see. (pp. 194-95)

The failure of the March pushes Bashra and his followers back into a reassertion of their mystical hopes of repatriation to Ethiopia, and Jerry is forced to recognize that he has failed to help the Brethren to become the third political party he has dreamed of. The failure of the march, and with it of

Jerry's hopes of 'the re-entry and rehabilitation of the thousands of members into the Island society' signals the beginning of the prophesied success of the Blood an' Thunder group. Their first revolt is crushed by the police with the usual violence, and the stage is set for yet another bitter, internal struggle in which Jamaican will maim Jamaican, a return to the bitter ease of hurting that Roger Mais had already so ably described. In a rather theatrical ending the Termites are killed in a car crash whilst returning from a 'pitch' up-country and Jerry is left to contemplate his failure and to wonder if 'someone with more experience [would] take over, and work at it?' It is clear, though unstated, that Jerry Stoker's next move will be the journey out from the islands to that exile which, though no solution, is at least a temporary ease to the pain of life in the troubled Caribbean.

Salkey's novel is often rambling and over-emphatic, drawing out its effects too generously, and capping over-long descriptions with a too-neat narrative comment. But as a study of island society from inside it is a significant attempt to uncover the possibilities open to a young West Indian who desires to come to terms with his time and place. Its valuable insight into the strange and uneasy alliances between black-power rhetoric and religious fanaticism in Jamaican society is not only prophetic but also serves as a pattern through which Salkey can make his readers aware of the difficulties in West Indian society of creating presents unsullied by the bitterness and fantasy inherited from the violent and disillusioned past. Its very overemphasis is a symptom of a seriousness which marks it as a significant step in the West Indian novel's attempt to become the reflector and shaper of its times. The scarcity of novels dealing with adult, contemporary life in the West Indies reflects the experience of the writers. Even Salkey's novel limits itself to the experience of men in their twenties, and ends with a potential flight. As we noted earlier, between 1950 and the mid-sixties there was a steady decrease in the number of books published in the West Indies, reflecting the increasing number of writers who had chosen to settle abroad. Although there have been signs recently that this situation may be slowly changing, with the younger writers choosing to remain at home, the present generation of established figures have spent all or most of their mature life outside the countries they write about. There is no parallel that I know to this situation. Elsewhere the expatriate writer is in a minority, often a large and fruitful one, but a minority nonetheless. In the West Indies he is the norm. With the increasing political unrest in Africa in the last few years the number of writers working temporarily or permanently outside their own countries has dramatically increased. But even here exile has not been, as in the West Indies, an almost inescapeable accompaniment to literary recognition and artistic success. As a result the characteristic novel dealing with the West Indian writer's reaction to contemporary life has been the novel of return from exile.

The novel dealing with the return of an expatriate figure forms, with the novels of childhood and of emigration a final stage in the experiential pattern of the West Indian writer, and its examples are as numerous and diverse. It is difficult to fix on its characteristics, though two must be mentioned: the protagonist is often a writer himself, though his function may not be very active in the story; and the island to which he returns is usually fictionalized to some degree or other. Perhaps this last feature illustrates the search for a detachment, a wider vision of experience, reflecting the writer's hope that he is now able to see the West Indies in a world context. Or, perhaps it is slightly defensive, though at a personal rather than a political level, since there are only one or two notable examples of exclusion or disfavour recorded so far.

George Lamming's novel *Of Age and Innocence* (1958)[19] may serve as an example, since it incorporates most of the common features and is also an exceptionally successful novel to boot. Lamming's fictionalized island, San Cristobal, is better realized than most, less easily identifiable as a mere pseudonym like Hearne's Cayuna (Jamaica) or Naipaul's Isabella (Trinidad). And this fact, insignificant in itself, reflects Lamming's success in creating a world which reflects the general experience of the West Indies, without losing the force of specific experience. This novel, the first of the San Cristobal novels, has been followed by three others which extend the study of this imaginary world: *Season of Adventure* (1960); *Water With Berries* (1971); and *Natives of My Person* (1972). Though I have, for the most part, tried to avoid following individual careers, and chronicling novels with any pretence at comprehensive coverage, it may be worth noting that both the first novels deal with contemporary life in San Cristobal. After the novel chronicling the fate of those who return to the island (*Of Age and Innocence*) Lamming attempts a novel set in and about the life of San Cristobal itself, (*Season of Adventure*) tracing the search for an identity which can reconcile the diverse heritage of the West Indies as symbolized in the figure of the girl Fola. The long silence which followed may, perhaps, reflect Lamming's own feeling that the attempt was not completely successful. Whatever the cause it is interesting to note that his next work (*Water with Berries*) deals with a group of San Cristobalians in exile in London, and the last (*Natives of My Person*) with a sixteenth century voyage which sets out in discovery of San Cristobal (the Islands of Black Rock). Perhaps this return to an historical root, which, incidentally, produces a powerful symbolic novel free in large part of the unnecessary complexities which so often interfere with Lamming's main conceptions in the earlier work, may prove to be an effective jumping off point for a fresh engagement with the here and now. The first of the series, *Of Age and Innocence*, is a boldly conceived, and largely successful, attempt to show the impact on a group of expatriates of the tensions and difficulties of modern West Indian life. Mark Kennedy, an expatriate writer returning home after years of exile in London is the central figure in a group of outsiders which include his English wife Marcia and his friends Bill and Penelope Butterfield. Returning to San Cristobal at the same time is Shephard, an expatriate whose homecoming heralds a wave of political action in the island in which Mark Kennedy becomes involved. The attempt to forge an effective society from the various racial and class groupings within the island is the skeleton of the action. This is the structure around which Lamming builds a series of detailed studies of the individual reactions of his characters to the events of their time. There is no solution proffered to the complexities they discover both in the society of San Cristobal and in themselves. But, as they react, the theme of the interaction of personal identity and a viable social expression is developed in a careful, and typically complex, counter-pointing of private and public incident. The investigation is deepened through a skilful and imaginative use of symbol and fable. Lamming uses the lives of the sons of some of the main characters as a parallel action, creating a pattern of responses to San Cristobal in which the reactions of innocence and maturity are compared. The sons of Shephard, of the Indian leader Singh, the Chinese Lee and the white police chief Crabbe form a tightly-knit group they call The Society. In their aspirations towards unity and friendship, and in the gradual intrusion of the inevitable divisions and jealousies as they explore their innocent world the problems of their elders are reflected and prefigured. In one of Lamming's most telling and economic uses of allegorical fable the boys are the mouthpieces for a legend which seems to sum up the tensions of San Cristobal, past, present and future. Their story of the Tribe Boys, the Bandit Kings and the Warrior Ants emphasizes and illustrates the historical origins of the divisiveness and economic greed which shapes so much of the experience of San Cristobal. The optimism of the boys and its gradual decline parodies the experience of their elders, emphasizing that innocence and its vision can only be preserved with difficulty and courage.

'My father say they goin' keep San Cristobal,' said Lee, 'like how we have the Society, but he don't know 'bout the Society, the way we three different an' still alike.'

> 'They talk 'bout the future like a war,' said Singh, 'how the future goin' come only with the struggle.'
> 'An' we have the future already,' said Lee, 'cause we make a little Society for three, an' we see how it work.'
> ' 'Tis cause they live so long before,' said Bob, 'that the future look hard to reach. But we reach already.'
> (p. 120)

At the end of the novel their disillusion reflects that of their elders, including Mark Kennedy's. They have had to learn that the system is complex and that deception, violence and fear are as available to the Law as to those who seek to change it. Bob, whose father Shephard has been betrayed and killed along with their friend Rowley, Crabbe's son, reflects that the struggle which had seemed so easy will be a long and bitter one.

> 'Tomorrow is the trial,' said Bob.
> 'Tomorrow an' maybe till a next tomorrow it last,' Singh said.
> 'But hardly more,' said Bob, 'tomorrow an' a next tomorrow.'
> Lee did not speak. (p. 412)

Of Age and Innocence is a successful attempt to disentangle some of the main issues confronting West Indian society and to try and define the nature and cost of a decision to alter it. The sources of doubt and self-confusion are shown to be implicit in the political and economic entanglements the races have inherited and from which they are unable to free themselves and their consciousness. In the reactions of all groups to the issues posed Lamming provides a very strong case against the racially based solutions to the West Indian problem. For him too the heart of the problem is in the past and the way in which it has shaped the possibilities for each individual. But no group is exempt, and no group is able to withdraw. If the problem is founded in the history of their past interactions the solution can only be found there too.

SECTION 4—NOTES

1. Introduction by the Hon. Norman W. Manley in *The Three Novels of Roger Mais*; Jonathan Cape; London, 1966; p. vi.
2. MOORE, Gerald, *The Chosen Tongue*; Longmans; London, 1969; p. 3.
3. *The Chosen Tongue* pp. 3-4.
4. REID, V.S., *New Day*; introd. Mervyn Morris; Caribbean Writers Series 4; Heinemann; London, 1973; p. i.
5. JAMES, Louis, *The Islands in Between*; OUP; London, 1968; p. 64.
6. REID, V.S., *New Day* p. 24.
7. *The Hills Were Joyful Together* (1953); *Brother Man* (1954) and *Black Lightning* (1955) – the three have been re-issued as *The Three Novels of Roger Mais*; Jonathan Cape; London, 1966; 2nd edition 1970. *Brother Man* was re-written just before Roger Mais' death. *Black Lightning* was hastily revised into its final form, but may be regarded as technically finished. Jean Creary records the existence of a 'last novel, *In the Sight of the Sun*, which exists only as a massive, unpublished fragment' but this I have not seen. All references are to the Jonathan Cape re-issue.
8. *The Hills Were Joyful Together* p. 71.
9. See, for example, Jean Creary's essay 'A Prophet Armed: The Novels of Roger Mais' in *The Islands in Between* ed. Louis James; pp. 50-63.
10. *The Hills Were Joyful Together* p. 12.
11. *The Hills Were Joyful Together* p. 226.
12. *The Hills Were Joyful Together* p. 288.
13. *Brother Man* in *Three Novels of Roger Mais* p. 109.
14. See also Andrew Salkey's novel *A Quality of Violence* for a parallel treatment of this theme in Jamaican life.
15. *Brother Man* p. 188.
16. MOORE, Gerald, *A Chosen Tongue*; Longmans; London, 1969; p. 7.
17. NAIPAUL, V.S., *A House for Mr. Biswas*; Penguin; London, 1969; p. 49.
18. SALKEY, Andrew, *The Late Emancipation of Jerry Stoker*; Hutchinson; London, 1968; p. 1.
19. LAMMING, George, *Of Age and Innocence*; Michael Joseph; London, 1958.

5

MYTH AND REALITY:
The Search for a Form

The growing interest from the sixties onwards in the new writing from Africa and the Caribbean reflects the general interest since the war in any writing which seems to offer new ways of approaching the problem of meaningful form. The initial reaction of European and American critics to the work of a writer like Amos Tutuola illustrates the point. Their concern is less with the significance of Tutuola's work in itself, or as a development of the complex, oral tradition of Yoruba literature, than with the 'originality' of its treatment of language or narrative form. In this 'originality', of course, they see the possibility of a renewal for the novel form, a revitalization of the European tradition. African critics, on the other hand, have been more alive to the traditional qualities of Tutuola's writing and the debt he owes to Yoruba story-telling forms and Yoruba mythology and legend.

This strong division in critical reaction to the work of Tutuola illustrates the hopes and fears of his readers. African critics, who speak out against the adulation accorded Tutuola in Europe and America, point to the stereotypical limitations of the work, and compare it unfavourably with the practice of traditional Yoruba tale-tellers, or with the work of modern writers who have remained faithful to Yoruba like D.O. Fagunwa; whilst European and American reactions swing erratically between an over-enthusiasm which hails such work as a stylistic salvation for the English language, and a subsequent denigration of its repetitiveness, lack of sequentiality and general formlessness. Such reactions more strongly reflect the disappointment of the critics' own hopes than their understanding of any alternative aesthetic which the form may reflect.

The links between the new writing in English from Africa and the Caribbean and the European literary traditions are undeniable. But they are also strictly limited. Only a full recognition of this will allow the European and American reader to understand the implications of these new literatures for his own culture. To begin with, in the case of African writing in English, there must be a frank realization that much of the originality of the writing stems from its relationship with traditional, oral literature. In this sense, some African critics have argued, there is no new or 'emerging' African writing, only a continuity of a literature which is already centuries old.[1] A full and fair assessment of the debt to oral traditions is difficult to make. The detailed study of the vast range of African oral literature is in its infancy. A whole generation of linguistic and anthropological studies have done no more than scratch the surface of what it has to offer. There is no doubt that the new generation of African scholars will address themselves to this task in a different spirit to that of their European predecessors, and in those studies so far published by African scholars there is a noticeable and welcome move to recognize the continuity of the oral traditions and contemporary written expression. Even where there is no immediate, large-scale oral literature, as in much of the Caribbean for example, there needs to be a clearer recognition that although the language employed is English, the experience recorded is not, and that the new experience may profoundly alter the language and the form employed.

But with these provisos it is equally clear that literature written in English will, whatever its place of origin, inevitably be influenced by the whole literature in that language. This is nowhere more obvious than in the wholesale adoption in

Africa and the Caribbean of the existing European genres. A novel in English wherever written and with whatever subject-matter will inevitably be influenced by the existing examples of the genre, even where that influence leads to a deliberate distortion or denial of the characteristic features.

The hope with which so many greeted the new writers from Africa and the Caribbean was that their new range of experience and their different cultural premises would invigorate and renew the forms they had inherited from Europe and America. To date it must be recorded that this has only happened to a limited degree. Again, perhaps, this was to be expected, and yet many critics have denied even the success that has been achieved.

It is quite natural that where the majority of writers are inexperienced there will be a glut of imitations and the emergence of a number of 'formulae' slavishly adhered to by the second rate, but there are also a number of excellent examples of each kind, and an increasing number of works which are breaking new ground, and extending year by year the possibilities of the situation. In addition, in assessing the achievement of this writing and the originality of its development it ought to be borne in mind that different aesthetic goals may need to be taken into account. The development of new forms has been the dominant European standard of excellence for most of the twentieth century but it is by no means universally accepted, and even in European circles many in our time have deplored the loss of a concept of art in which form exists outside the impulses of the individual artist, and in which excellence is measured by the skill with which he executes the task of remaking and renewing the perfected ideal. With the renewed interest in traditional aesthetics, we may see African writers aiming more towards these ideals of renewal and increasingly rejecting the built-in cultural obsolescence of much recent European and American fiction. But for the most part the work done so far in English in Africa and the Caribbean has been conventional in its acceptance of the traditions of the European genres.

Indeed, the response has often seemed old-fashioned by contemporary European and American standards. An obvious reason for this is in the models available. Most African writers have taken their examples of the form from traditional English literature courses, and critics in the early period were delighted to recognize this and to play the game of spotting the influences. African writers have been frank in acknowledging these borrowings: Achebe has spoken of the effect on him of a reading of Conrad; Ngugi acknowledges a debt to Lawrence; whilst Okigbo's early verse is replete with homages to Eliot, Pound and Yeats, as well as to the Greek and Roman writers he studied at the University. Perhaps it is this which accounts for the rather old-fashioned, or as it has more kindly and more accurately been described, 'classical' feel of much of the writing: the solidity, for example, and the assurance of Achebe; the rich, symbolic texture of Lamming; or the detailed ironic observation of V.S. Naipaul. Other influences obviously play their part, not least the oral traditions mentioned above. But it remains largely true that African and West Indian writers have been able to use forms which their English and American contemporaries have felt to be closed to them; or, at least, available only within some distancing framework of irony or parody.

The social framework of this writing provides part of the explanation. From the beginning, as I have tried to show, the African and Caribbean writer saw that he had an important role to play in shaping the consciousness of his people. His work was designed not only to record his experience, but also to renew his countrymen's awareness of their own unique identity. In the case of the African writer this was further reinforced by the traditional function of the artist in many African societies, and the stress laid in traditional aesthetics on the social value of art rather than on individual expression. All this meant that the writer was always aware that his art was defined, in part, by its function in the world he described. Hence, subject-matter assumed an importance in itself. At its best this has led to a sense that this writing deals with the real world in a simple and frank way which Western writers may envy; at its worst it has led to the dangerous assumption that form is unimportant and that the only task of the writer is to be honest in the face of his experience and his beliefs. It is this simplistic attitude which leads to the merely autobiographical works, or the sketchy journalism of the worst writing from these areas. But, where this attitude of commitment to one's time and place has gone hand in hand with a respect for form, and an understanding of the intimate connection between style and content in good writing it has led to a revitalization of traditional forms in prose and verse, and, more recently, to creative and innovative experiment with the inherited European genres. Writers like Achebe, Okigbo, Okara and Awoonor in Africa, or Mais, Reid, Selvon and Lamming in the Caribbean have, as I have tried to show, continually developed new techniques designed to accommodate English to the new experiences drawn from African and West Indian social life. Their work shows, beyond a doubt, the range of achievement and innovation this special double relationship of language and culture can create. But I want now to consider the work of two writers who stand out as examples of those who have explored through a substantial body of work the full implication for the European genres of their transplantation into cultures other than that which shaped them: Wole Soyinka, of Nigeria; and Wilson Harris, of Guyana.

Soyinka's work covers the whole range of literary genres, poetry, plays, two novels, a wide range of essays and critical articles. His early and much anthologized poem *Telephone Conversation* is still a good introduction to his peculiar and attractive combination of humour, bitterness and deeply-felt commitment to the cause of the individual and personal in a world in love with labels of colour, race, and politics. Though, interestingly, Soyinka omits it from his later collections perhaps, as Eldred Jones suggests, because he feels it is not representative of his work as a whole, even though as late as *The Interpreters* (1965) he shows the same capacity for wickedly exact humorous observation of the behaviour of the snobbish and the bigoted.[2]

Even in this early poem we can see how sensitive Soyinka is to the shades of tone and accent in dialogue, and it is not surprising, perhaps, that his greatest success has been as a dramatist. Drama has been something of the poor relation in West African writing. Writers have tended to produce a one-off play and have not, with the odd exception, produced a body of work for the theatre. The main problem was the difficulty of reconciling the elements of European and African performance traditions.

Performance arts in traditional society, as one might expect, centred on music, dance and oratory (recited verse) rather than on imitated action tied to a dramatic 'text'.[2] It was Soyinka who first realized that in this 'difficulty' lay an opportunity to develop a play-form in which spoken dialogue could resume its ancient role as a single, vital, but not exclusive element in performance. Soyinka saw that to wed existing performance 'skills' to a more representational and sequential European dramatic 'form' required the existence of new performers as well as new writers. Soyinka's earliest play performances were staged in London where he spent from 1957-1959 as Play Reader at the Royal Court theatre. In 1959 he had two plays staged in Ibadan, Nigeria, including the popular *The Lion and the Jewel*, a study of the relations between traditional values and the impulse to modernize in Nigerian village society. But it was in 1960 that he made a commitment to theatre in a deeper sense when he set up his first 'company' in Nigeria. This company, 'The 1960 Masks', produced *A Dance of the Forests*, the play Soyinka wrote to celebrate Nigerian Independence. Although fragments of this work had been written earlier, and even shown at the Royal Court in 1959, the play is clearly conceived not just as a text, but as a vehicle through which the new company could create a style. In the play a subtle and complex text is wedded to traditional performance skills and patterns. The result is a unique expression of the meeting point of two cultures. In time I am sure that the first production of *A Dance of the Forests* at the Independence Celebrations in Lagos in October 1960 will come to be seen as a date as important to theatre in Africa as the publication of Achebe's *Things Fall Apart* has been to the African novel.

The play's basic structure is deceptively simple. Two worlds, widely separated in time, are joined through the transitional world of the bush of ghosts (compare Tutuola, *My Life in the Bush of Ghosts*), that forest of Yoruba mythology in which living and dead may join in the communion of action. The first world, that of modern Nigeria, is represented by a town gathered together for celebration, an obvious parallel to the Celebrations for which the play was written. As traditionally prescribed, such a celebration must invoke not only those who are alive, but through them and their rituals the ancestors from whom they are descended, and whose life still flows through their activities. The gods or daemons of the forest are representatives of that alternative world to the world of the living, which in traditional Yoruba myth forms a transition or bridge between the living and the dead. Through their intervention two of the 'dead' are revived to represent the ancestors at the feast. Each of these are figures who have interacted with the spirits of the main living protagonists in their earlier incarnations in the past. The past world Soyinka depicts is based on one of the ancient Sudanic kingdoms from which the contemporary Yoruba is descended. This world, which Soyinka calls the court of Mata Kharibu, parallels the contemporary world of the Yoruba township, showing that despite their differences, past and present share a continuous pattern of human effort, pain, cruelty, and achievement. Within this simple yet highly dramatic framework Soyinka weaves a pattern of responses which insists on the continual interdependence of past and present. His 'message' is no simple social one. Like any good dramatist he is primarily concerned to show a process in action, a process which, by implication, defines the limits of possibility for the human characters who act out its events.

His stress on images of recurrence and continuity has a positive and a negative aspect. Renewal, symbolized by the celebrations, is always possible, but only within the recurrent limitations of human response, which is shown to be bitterly similar in its possibilities and its frustrations from generation to generation. The returning dead man and dead woman (pregnant at her death centuries before, and yearning to deliver her burden into this new world) discover those they knew at the court of Mata Kharibu plying their old trades with the same lustfulness and cunning in this new world. Rola, the prostitute, was in their time the notorious courtesan Madame Tortoise; Demoke, the Court Poet of Mata Kharibu, is still an artist, the town carver; Adenebi, the Court Historian, is now the Town Council Orator; while Agboreko, Mata Kharibu's Soothsayer is the so-called Elder of Sealed Lips, still half-politician, half-charlatan. The clear application of this pattern to the new society for whose independence the play was staged could not have been lost on its original audience. Its message is a warning one. Not in essence a denial of the possible benefits which might accrue, but a graphic statement in image and character of the inflexibility of the human stuff from which dreams of progress must be made.

As important as this 'message' is the innovatory technique Soyinka develops to communicate it. For example the Half-Child offspring of the reborn Dead Woman from the ancestral past, is a symbol which serves as a catalyst to gather together many of the strands of implication in the action. The final impact of this symbol is not made in literary terms. Throughout the play Soyinka has written in possibilities for extending the dialogue through music, dance and mime. Here in the climax, the fate of the Half-Child, a difficult and intricate symbolic resolution of the action, is rendered not in speech but in an adaptation of traditional dance and game.

The printed text offers two versions of this ending, one as produced at Lagos in 1960 and a second which forms part of the text Soyinka later published. The two are interestingly different, mainly in the degree to which the printed version suggests the use of a specific and highly dangerous seeming dance which Soyinka refers to as the 'dance of the child acrobats', in which Half Child is tossed into the air and, apparently, caught on the point of two knife blades. In the version as staged by the 1960 Masks this is amended to the tossing of an *ibeji* totem doll. Are we entitled to assume that Soyinka as director had discovered that the people who were available to form a new theatre company in Nigeria did not possess all the skills of a traditional dance troupe? If so, then it suggests that a period of transition would be required, and a process of adaptation be necessary. Traditional performance techniques would form the inspiration for the new troupes, but the alternative theatrical skills they would need to cope with a formal script might well preclude their simultaneous mastery of the more elaborate traditional performance skills. As with so much else in modern Africa the new theatre forms would of necessity be a blending of old and new, a synthesis rather than a restoration. Nor need this be a bad thing, since as Soyinka goes on to show the new forms which have emerged may develop the possibilities of both source traditions. Soyinka has commented on the difficulties he encountered in creating a professional company in Nigeria; and the unusual practice of training professionals within an amateur structure which he adopted in the early sixties.

> I returned to Nigeria for the first time in four and a half years – in 1960 ... the first thing I wanted to do was to get my own company together. There were many ways in which this could be done. I could move towards trying to establish a full theatre from the very beginning, but there were many factors which militated against this: lack of money, and then there was the training problem because this was in January, 1960, and I wanted the company to be ready – say, in October, 1960 – when we would stage a production for the Independence

Celebration. I very badly wanted to do this because we could obtain money for that if we managed to swing the other. So I rejected what was to start a company from scratch: young semi-professional people, and go through the process of training and so on. We had to make do instead with those who'd had enormous acting experience.[3]

This company, the 1960 Masks, were as Soyinka goes on to explain 'mainly of the middle class civil servant types, you know, who had senior service jobs, were very comfortable ...' Apart from the obvious logistic difficulties in reconciling commitment to the theatre with demanding professional commitments these people were unable to exercise a critical dimension effectively since their livelihood was tied to government organizations. For this reason Soyinka declares he was dissatisfied with this theatre even though 'when we were ready to produce a play the result was quite satisfactory.' As he puts it,

> ... this was not the theatre I wanted, and from the beginning they understood that they were there to encourage a new younger group of fully professional actors and actresses. And from the beginning they never took any money at all. What little money we had went to three or four people whom we began training right underneath the major productions, increasing their number as time went on. They understood this really was to become the theatrical company, and they were very generous, they really loved what they were doing ...
> (*In Person* p. 96)

The new company which gradually emerged from the 1960 Masks was the Orisun Theatre Company It was with this group that Soyinka was able to explore the new techniques which gave rise to plays like *Kongi's Harvest* and *The Road* (1965), plays which fully develop the integrated use of traditional performance skills and complex verbal symbols.

At the heart of this development is Soyinka's use of traditional features. From *A Dance of the Forests* (1963) to *Madmen and Specialists* (1971) this is never nostalgic nor motivated by narrow cultural chauvinism. Rather it is the attempt to discover through traditional features the actual living languages (rituals) by which modern Nigerian consciousness can be shaped.

In the lecture quoted above Soyinka clearly defines the dangers he sees to be present in the process of mythic and ritual reconstruction and points towards a more dynamic use of ritual directed *towards* change *through* reintegration. It should be understood that Soyinka is here addressing an audience of Americans, and his remarks are therefore directed immediately towards the problems of black American writers.

> There has been, as you must all be aware, a very serious search among black writers for an idiom which would serve not only to rejuvenate the arid conditions of European theatricality but which would serve to integrate the fragmented and even distorted consciousness of the black people in the midst of a domineering culture. The search has led them inevitably back to the mother continent in a desperate hunt for ritual into the very liturgy of traditional drama. It has bred some distortions, some superficiality, created even comic melodrama where none is intended. This search should be understood as going backwards into that recombining essence of ritualism from which drama emerged. Drama, I think we have agreed, is by its nature a revolutionary art form. It is not therefore accidental that an exploration into the basic idioms of expression has been most manifest in drama on this continent, the black section of it. The dangers have been stated, and it is possible that once the reasons for this urge are understood, the most opposite form for the social reality here may be discovered in the existing ritual idioms which are on the

spot and not necessarily those which are borrowed from Africa. (*In Person* pp. 75-6)

What Soyinka seems to be asserting is the continuity between the historical root of ritual and its function both in the community and in the individual which that community nourishes. Quoting Fanon he continues,

> Franz Fanon writes:
> 'The atmosphere of myth and magic frightens me and so takes on an undoubted reality. By terrifying me it integrates me into the traditions and the history of my district or of my tribe and at the same time it reassures me, it gives me a status as it were, an identification paper. The occult sphere is a sphere belonging to the community which is entirely under magical jurisdiction. By entangling myself into the inextricable network where actions are repeated with crystalline inevitability, I find the everlasting world which belongs to me and the perenniality which is thereby affirmed of the world belonging to us.'
> And for the dramatist who seeks to integrate myth and ritual into the revolutionary potential of a play, these words contain their own warning. The network is inextricable, the matrix of which the ritual form is merely a shell, is a perennial one, an intricate evolution from tradition and history, not merely of myth and magic alone. Ritual therefore contains its own stringent dialectic; it is not merely a visual, decorative framework.
> (*In Person* pp. 76-7)

It is in the active and dynamic integration of traditional myth and practice with contemporary concerns that Soyinka's distinctive contribution lies. In his work we see the possibility of a creative collaboration between traditional and modern elements. Thus, for example, the Half-Child of *A Dance of the Forests* has its roots in the Yoruba myth of the *Abiku*, the child which cannot rest in either the world of the living or the dead, and which returns to be born again and again to the anguish of the mother who can neither prevent its conception nor succeed in keeping it alive. But this myth which informs the final scene of the play is only the starting point for a dramatized action whose meaning is not limited by its source. Thus the *abiku* child image unites with all the other devices in the play, including the structural skeleton of past, present and spirit worlds of action, as a complex image of the continuity of human limitations and human frustrations within the developing Nigerian experience. Most critical discussion of Soyinka's work has dealt with the plays of the early and middle period quite fully, so I should prefer to concentrate on two of the later plays in which we can see the mature result of these experiments in blending distinct structures and performance traditions into a new and individual theatre style: *The Road* (1965) and *Madmen and Specialists* (1971).

To define the achievement of Soyinka in a play like *The Road* it is necessary to emphasize again the 'revolutionary' aim of his use of traditional features. The purpose of the play is not merely to illustrate the continuity between the ritual forms of the traditional culture and the modes of contemporary experience, but to forge from their interaction a tool which can change the audience's awareness of an experience they all share. Such a drama seeks to draw together *all* the systems through which contemporary experience can be understood and out of which it has grown. This may involve the exposure of alternative, e.g. imported and alien, systems as inadequate interpretative tools. Thus, in *The Road* Christianity is exposed as a limiting and stultifying system where it has led to the suppression of concepts which its symbols cannot handle; and yet it is a portion of the available languages and rituals through which the existing situation has been shaped, and so has a part to play in any response to it. Soyinka has defined the process as follows:

> We are emphasizing the sensitive adoption of what has become integrated within the cultural matrix of a

society – whatever and wherever it is – into the idiom of the ritual for making new social and, we hope, revolutionary statements. (*In Person* p. 85)

This process emphasizes a use of the actual rituals alive in the sensitivities of ordinary people now. Soyinka's purpose, he has said, is to 'find a creative mode which would not be coming downwards from a very imaginary creative ideal, to find a language which expresses the right source of thought and values, and merges them with symbols of contemporary reality or fuses them into a universal idiom such as ritual.' Sensitive to the danger of misconstruction, Soyinka is careful to avoid any confusion of his concept with facile cultural or political slogans. He finishes his statement with a warning, and a refusal of simplifications.

The creative ideal in revolutionary theatre is not a self-conscious pandering to any proletarian illusion on any level whatever, be it the spiritual level or the social-revolutionary level because, as we have said, the matrix of creativity, most especially in the dramatic mode, embraces at all times – both in individual and communal effectiveness – the regenerative potential of society. And it is not the immediate definable or tangible but the inherent potential of society – technological, political, artistic etc … that constitutes the totality of a people's culture. (*In Person* pp. 87-8)

It is this aim which we have to keep in mind when we approach the structure and imagery of *The Road*. Symbols of contemporary reality (the road, accidental death, motor vehicles, signposts, hit and run accidents) are fused with the ritual implications of traditional symbols (the dog sacrifice to Ogun, the agemo mark, the ritual gourd and libation) to create a language which is able fully to realize the significance of death in the modern Nigerian context, and which points the way to a creative regeneration of the *whole* view of the culture in the face of death.

The heart of the play is the search of the Professor for a symbol capable of expressing the meaning of death in the world he inhabits. His initial term for this symbol, the Word, is of course Christian. Professor, we discover, is a disgraced lay preacher who has been cast out by the Christian community. It becomes clear that his disgrace involves drink, appropriation of church funds, and a general rejection of the dogma and ethics of the Christian community. But these actions are also expressions of the Professor's rejection at a deeper level of the adequacy of the Word, since the Christian concept is an inadequate expression of the cultural imperatives working through him. The Christian symbol is unable to express actions and ideas which are an essential part of the Professor's Yoruba identity. Thus, for example, Christian puritanism rejects the wholeness of the Yoruba concept of life, in which the maimed, broken and inadequate are an expression of the weakness of the God of creation, Obatala. For the Yoruba, Obatala *can* incorporate weakness, *can* be drunk and inadequate even as he symbolizes creativity and strength; a sustaining contradiction which is typical of the dialectic comprehensiveness of the Yoruba idea of creativity and force. Similarly, in the simple division of life and death the Christian system excludes the rich complexity of the tripartite world of Yoruba myth in which a transitional, 'unborn', or 'undead' state may supplement and coexist with the world of living and dead. Not only the Christian framework, but even the technological framework of the contemporary world seems to reject this wholeness. The concept of a road accident, an accidental death, fractures the idea of wholeness, suggesting as it does an oversight, a moment of neglect, rather than a fruitful insight into the inevitable pattern of life and death as a sustaining and necessary part of a whole process. Again the Christian technological culture disrupts the notion of the continuity of destruction and creation, symbolized for a Yoruba by the God Ogun, who is both creator and destroyer, and whose contradictory impulses are ritualized in the idea of sacrifice/

libation, the destruction of part of the whole to bring forth the whole.

What Soyinka does is to present an action in which characters and audience can trace the growth of an alternative series of rituals through which the full meaning of an event in the whole context of this culture can be explored. This alternative mythos is both celebrated by and created through the developing action of the play.

This action centres on an accident which has occurred before the play begins. Kotonu, a mammy-wagon driver and his passenger-tout Samson have killed the masked celebrant of a Driver's Festival, dedicated to the God Ogun. This festival involves the sacrifice of a dog. This reflects the general Nigerian practice of running down dogs as a propitiatory sacrifice to Ogun [the god of drivers] who, as we noted above, also represents the meeting point of destruction and creation, the transitional ground out of which each is renewed. Kotonu has never been able to propitiate the god in the normal way, though Samson has warned him that his scruples are dangerous

> ... When other drivers go out of the way to kill a dog, Kotonu nearly somersaults the lorry trying to avoid a flea-racked mongrel. Why, I ask him, why? Don't you know a dog is Ogun's meat? Take warning Kotonu. Before it's too late take warning and kill us a dog.[4]

Kotonu's victim has been brought to the bar-cum-spare-parts store of the Professor, and has disappeared. Kotonu, we learn, has been unable to continue as a driver since the accident and has sought out the Professor and his dumb-servant Murano in a bid to understand the meaning of the accident, and to achieve, presumably, some form of expiation. All this information is revealed gradually and in a non-sequential way. Thus the details of the accident are presented not as related, past information in a neo-Aristotelian way, but in the form of an eruption into the action of a re-enactment of the scene. Since the original festival was itself a re-enactment of an event not expressible in other terms the presentation of this event on stage is achieved by a parallel re-enactment, not a mere dramatized commentary. Thus the action of the play flows from actual to ritual event just as life itself flows from the actual (the present and living) to the ritual (the co-existent and spiritual) event in the Yoruba conception of existence. This process makes the structure difficult to grasp at first, though the play is very clearly and openly constructed with no deliberate confusion or opaqueness. An example of the method in action may make the process clearer:

At the beginning of Act Two Samson repeats his pleading with Kotonu to 'kill us a dog', again warning that 'The one who won't give Ogun willingly will yield heavier meat by Ogun's designing.' (p. 59) As the Act develops we realize that this is not just a repetition of the warnings which Kotonu ignored prior to the accident but a plea that he should sacrifice now to prevent Ogun demanding his right later in some other form. Kotonu's refusal throughout seems to be based on a respect for life which is totally acceptable within the Christian framework, but is dangerous and foolish within the Yoruba conception that a flow from life to death is a necessary and inevitable part of the structure of existence. The Professor insists that the Christian Word is inadequate, an illusion when seen as a sufficient explanation. Thus he variously describes it as 'a blasphemy' (p. 68), as 'not the Word' (p. 68) and as only 'the first illusion of the Word' (p. 69). The Christian concept of the Word is inadequate because it cannot contain the wholeness of Yoruba conceptions, symbolized in the play by *agemo*, a cult of the dissolution of the flesh. This cult symbolizes the importance of a transitional phase between life and death, a place of meeting from which there are 'doorways' from one world to the next. These doorways, which include sacrifices (e.g. 'accidental' deaths) are a necessary part of the renewing process of life. The elements of the Christian Word which approach this conception (e.g. in the midst of life we are in death; died so that we should have eternal life; the grain of wheat that must rot in the ground to bring forth new shoots) are a partial symbolizing of what in the Yoruba mythos finds a fuller expression in the *agemo* cult, in the Ogun practices and in the ritual libations and sacrifices associated with these. Since Kotonu is Yoruba, only a ritual which incorporates those mysteries which are his own can properly slake his need. One thing needs to be made quite clear; the play is not a polemic in favour of Nigerian versus Christian cult practices but an enactment of the psychic and spiritual inadequacy of any ritual which does not grow out of the whole range of sources which inform those who celebrate them. This point is made not through the dialogue, but through the enactment on stage of Kotonu and Samson's inability to escape these needs within themselves. The verbal symbol, 'the Word' is shown to be inadequate by the Professor's comments, and his continuing search for a 'Word' which will be adequate. But that Word will have to be made flesh in terms of a different sacrifice, in this case, the requisite sacrifice to Ogun. Thus when the Professor finishes his disquisition, an action erupts which reinforces his meaning and extends it.

> PROF: For the day will come, oh yes it will. Even atonement wilts before the Word ...
> [Samson breaks free with desperate strength, flees up-stage only to be met by the explosive fall of the tailboard. Right on the sound the light changes, leaving only the store area in light. Falling grotesquely after the board, is the mask. A moment later, Kotonu emerges from behind the mass of junk and clothing. Immediately, the mask-followers fill the stage searching for their mask-bearer. Kotonu stands dazed but Samson quickly raises the board and pushes the mask under it. It is a Driver's festival and they are all armed with whips and thick fibre stalks. Two carry a dog tied to a stake and brandish matchets. Dashing everywhere with the steady leader-and-refrain-chant they break off sporadically for brief

mutual whipping contests, dashing off again in pursuit.]

SAMSON: [as soon as they disappear.]: Help me lift him on board.

KOTONU: You saw it. Nothing could have saved him.

SAMSON: Come on come on.

KOTONU: It's all your fault. You said we should come.

SAMSON: That is neither here nor there. Let's hide him before they return.

KOTONU: But it wasn't my fault. Nothing could have saved him.

SAMSON: For heaven's sake man help me carry him up.

KOTONU: You know my reflexes are good Samson, but the way he ran across ...

SAMSON: They'll be back this way again.

KOTONU: But what was he running from? It was almost as if he was determined to die. Like those wilful dogs getting in the way of the wheels.

SAMSON: I am not the police Kotonu. Neither are those people. They talk with matchets. Across the throats – matchets!

KOTONU: Did you ask me here to be their butcher? You saw him, the way he fled across. Just tell me, was I to be part of this?

SAMSON: [manhandles the figure into the lorry and replaces the tailboard.]: Now get in and START THE ENGINE!

KOTONU: It's probably stalled.

SAMSON: What kind of talk is that? Have you gone mad? You haven't even tried man.

KOTONU: But it wasn't my fault.

SAMSON: [peers into the distance.]: They are coming again. Kotonu, for the last time!

KOTONU; Let me look underneath the mask.

SAMSON: Have you gone mad ... too late anyway, they've filled the road. But run at least. Come on let's run!

KOTONU: But who is he? Why did he run across?
SAMSON: You're hopeless. [Hurriedly he pulls down the tarpaulin.]
   But at least don't give us away. Look as if we are part of the festival. If there is danger one of us will have to get inside the mask. Do you understand?
   [Dumbly, Kotonu nods. The maskers come in again, performing the dance of the whips, darting off again and back, looking for the missing god.
   One of them dashes suddenly to the lorry and lifts up the tarpaulin. With desperate speed Samson snatches a whip from the nearest person and gives him a cut across the legs. The man readily accepts the invitation, and a contest follows.]
SAMSON: [shouts above the din.]: Now Kotonu, now! [Kotonu hesitates, visibly frightened.] Kotonu! Strip the mask and get under it! Kotonu it's the only way. [As if suddenly wakened, Kotonu starts, climbs into the lorry. The whip-dance grows fast and furious. Samson manoeuvres himself near the tailboard from time to time.]
   Hurry Kotonu! For heaven's sake hurry!
   [There is a sudden violent movement against the canvas and Samson, scared, rushes there. Almost at the same time, the masquerade comes through in violent throes, a figure in torment. There is a loud yell from the dancers and the whipping and chanting becomes more violent, aiding the god's seeming possession.]
KOTONU [tearing at the clothes, demented.]: It's all wet inside, I've got his blood all over me. [They dance and whip one another round the masquerade, leaving a clear space for his frenzy.] It's getting dark Samson I can't see. His blood has got in my eyes. I can't see Samson. [Samson, wildly irresolute, battles on with his latest challenger.] Samson where are you? My eyes are all clammed up I tell you. Samson! Samson! Samson!

[His struggles become truly frantic, full of violent contortions. Gradually he grows weaker and weaker, collapsing slowly on the ground until he is completely inert. The dancers flog one another off the scene.
A slow black-out, and a half-minute pause.
They are all back to normal. Enter Particulars Joe.]
PARTIC. JOE: Did he come in here?
(*The Road* pp. 70-73)

This action is not a 'flashback', but a re-enactment through the characters of Kotonu and Samson of their continuing unslaked need. The blood on Kotonu is not only the blood of the victim of the road accident but also the required libation necessary to readjust the offence to Ogun. The man killed wearing the mask is both man and god, and we gradually realize that Murano, Professor's servant, is this figure, dead and not dead, killed in the flesh, but alive in the spirit, an embodiment of that transitional phase between life and death which all men enter and which is ritually invoked when man takes upon himself the spirit of the god when he dons his mask. Someone else must 'get under the mask' in a different sense, must make that journey to the transitional world if the disturbance is to be readjusted. As the Act progresses it becomes clearer that Murano is the killed mask-bearer, and when he emerges clothed in the egungun mask he enters as himself and also as Ogun come to require the completion of the disturbed sacrifice, a sacrifice Kotonu might have made on the Road if he had followed Samson's advice and killed Ogun's meat. Now the price is heavier, and in the struggle with the masked spirit the Professor is inadvertently stabbed and dies. Once again the presentation of this final scene emphasizes the fact that happening and re-enactment are indissolubly wedded in this structure, since the final action is not just a struggle between characters resulting in an 'accidental' death, but also a sacrifice which completes the required ritual. Through that ritual the play asserts the cyclical continuity of creation and destruction which is the 'fulfilled Word' the Professor seeks. Thus as the thug Say Tokyo Kid and the Professor struggle the Mask (Murano/Ogun) is engaged in the spinning, circling dance to the *agemo* drum rhythm which the Professor has commanded his followers to beat, as he does every evening in the 'evening service'. With the arrival of Kotonu and Samson the time has come for the cycle to be completed, and their offence is re-enacted ritually when Say Tokyo Kid breaks the sacrificial gourd of palm-wine, provoking the Mask in a re-enactment of Kotonu's offence. Professor's death is thus both an 'accidental' event and a ritual fulfilment of the omitted sacrifice. The spinning, turning dance of the Mask visually re-enacts the meaning of Professor's death; just as in *agemo* cult practice it symbolizes the necessary continuity of death and life, of destruction and creation. Thus the death restores an order, not only philosophically, but ritually, insisting in both ways on that continuity of the living and the dead, of growth and dissolution which *agemo* celebrates. When the mask sinks at the end 'until it appears to be nothing beyond a heap of cloth and raffia' (p. 96) the renewal of this awareness has been completed intellectually and ritually.

However, it is necessary to emphasize that there has been a 'real' death in terms of the events recorded in the action. Professor dies in fact, within the narrative action of the play, and not just ritually. This emphasizes the 'revolutionary' content of Soyinka's action since it points to the manner in which such resolutions may be avoided. Professor's death has not resulted from the 'anger of a god' in any merely superstitious sense. It is expressive of the result of Kotonu's inability to understand his actions in terms of his whole personal identity. Thus, in the re-enactment of the ritual there is not only a reassertion but a regeneration, an action which indicates the relatedness of past and present and which points to more fully satisfactory means of synthesizing the two in the future. The play's action points not just to recovery, but to change through recovery.

The function of traditional material in Soyinka's work is

never merely illustrative, as *The Road* makes clear. A superficial glance at the progress of Soyinka's style would suggest a decreasing use of traditional material, nowhere more apparent than in a play like *Madmen and Specialists* (1971). But this conclusion needs to be modified in the light of Soyinka's expressed views on the function of traditional images and techniques. *Madmen and Specialists* (1971) is an African play, rooted in the contemporary Nigerian experience of war between conflicting ideologies and groups. But the theme is, of course, a universal one in the twentieth century. The African identity of the treatment is not the result of local or topical references, though these are present when they have a specific function [e.g. in rooting the play's metaphors in a specific historical soil relevant to the audience as in the Blindman's parody of a political speech at the end of Act 2 – though even here Soyinka seems as much concerned with pinning the parody on the particular audience watching as with establishing the play's Africanness, as his note makes clear: 'The speech should be varied with the topicality and locale of the time']; rather, it is in the development of alternative values which incorporate the insight of traditional wisdom. These symbolize the way modern 'specialists' overlook whole areas of their own make-up which should inform and guide their understanding of the world. Thus Bero, the specialist in medical 'control' is opposed by the old women, Iya Agba and Iya Mata, whose strength is drawn from traditional Yoruba healing practices – the gathering of herbs, the 'control' of nature by ritual act etc. The opposition of Bero and his fellow 'specialists' to this aspect of the world's wholeness is, therefore, symbolic of the self-destructive and rootless narrowness of many aspects of technological modernity. It would be foolish to debate whether the symbol is of a divorce of modern man from his past or of modern Nigeria from its traditions, since the one involves the other in the particular social and cultural matrix the play seeks to express and change. An even more telling example, because it functions through a reversed parody worthy of a Swift, is the use of the image of cannibalism as a logical extension of the practices of 'specialists' in modern war. Historically, the cannibal myth haunts the European psyche, not the African. It stands as a symbol of the projection of European libidinous fantasies into the African mind. Thus it is doubly ironic that Soyinka should use it as a symbol for the corruption of African values by the individual egotism which alienated modern man substitutes for communal loyalties and human intercourse; if the African seeks to recreate himself in the warped image of the modern European 'specialist' he must be ready to accept the whole package, Kurtz along with Conrad.

The characters of *Madmen and Specialists* are the broken remnants of war; cripples, spastics, blind and mad. Again, Soyinka has elected to explore an action the primary events of which occur before the play begins. As the action unfolds we learn of a revolt by Bero's father, the Old Man, in which he has served a modern Atrean feast to the specialists of modern war, including his own son. There is an inescapable 'logic' in his action. His 'madness' lies only in his acceptance of the price of war in dead and maimed, and in his view that to consume the dead to alleviate hunger and pain is only a natural extension of what exists. As the cause, so the consequence. This 'logic' (reminiscent of Arden's *Sergeant Musgrave's Dance*) is, of course, false. And yet, it points to a concept of total limited purpose by which any action can be justified which fascinates the 'specialists' even as it appals them. Bero, the son, inherits his father's madness in a 'specialised' form; cannibalism becomes an experience which 'liberates' him into a total amorality which reinforces his belief in the power of one man over another in the name of whatever the powerful choose to worship. (As It Was Now, As Ever Shall Be). But unlike the Madmen he must strive consciously to identify his ego with this justification of his own excess. This struggle manifests itself in the imprisonment of the Old Man and Bero's demand that he reveal to him 'the meaning of As'. But, of course, the specialist cannot penetrate the non-existent mystery. As is the ultimate predicate, and can be run through any alphabet of concepts. When Bero has rushed out in anger at the Old Man's ironic and mocking refusal to disclose the secret, the liberating name in which all abuse will be permissible, the Old Man begins his long desperate catechism of the Non-Existent.

> ... As Is, and the System is its mainstay though it wear a hundred masks and a thousand outward forms. And because you are within the System, the cyst in the System which irritates, the foul gurgle of the cistern, the expiring function of a faulty cistern and are part of the material for re-formulating the mind of a man into the necessity of the moment's political As, the moment's scientific As, metaphysic As, sociologic As, economic, recreative, ethical As you-cannot-es-cape! There is but one constant in the life of the System and that constant is AS ...[5]

The Old Man in his Madness has recognized a profounder 'truth' than that which Bero seeks to wrest from him. Man is capable of any evil if he does it in the name of an image which he can substitute for himself and use to absolve himself from responsibility. As is any metaphoric projection of ego into system; it is the ultimate excuse for the human abuse of self and others; the ultimate weapon against that human wholeness which dissolves when man divides himself into human and more than human, into priest and victim, into eater and eaten.

> ... you cyst, you cyst, you splint in the arrow of arrogance, the dog in dogma, tick of a heretic, the tick in politics, the mock of democracy, the mar of Marxism, a tick of the fanatic, the boo in buddhism, the ham in Mohammed, the dash in the criss-cross of Christ, a dot on the i of ego, an ass in the mass, the ash in ashram, a boot in kibbutz, the pee of priesthood, the peepee of perfect priesthood, or how dare you raise your hindquarters you dog of dogma and cast the scent of your existence in the lamp-post of Destiny you HOLE IN

THE ZERO of NOTHING! (*Madmen and Specialists* p. 76)

Bero's belief that he (his ego) can *use* As-ness to control others and himself is exposed in this tirade as idiocy. The egotism of the 'specialist' is destroyed in the Madman's comprehension that man is a parasite in the skin of his own fantasies and projections. But is this the 'truth' that the play as a whole offers? Is the Old Man a prophet or a madman? Does the play offer only a madman's cynicism as an alternative to the blind fanaticism of the specialists? The rejection of the madman's message seems to me to come in the form of a dramatic image rather than in argued dialogue and so may be overlooked, at least on the page, unless we take Soyinka's special technique into account. Before the 'war' (itself by now clearly an image of a wider and more continuous disruption in the nature of modern society itself) father and son had both been doctors. The suffering of the war has driven the Old Man into the perverted 'logic' of his doctrine of As and his son into his 'specialism' (a medical interrogator in the Intelligence Service, probing and controlling men's minds by drugs and surgery). But both have suffered this change because of the implicit values in their original lives, their essentially modern concept of healing as a single, individual and logical event, separated from wider contexts of negation and necessary suffering. Seeking universal security they have created universal suffering. An alternative to their perverted values must come from a world not merely opposed to their current beliefs in practice but based on quite different premises to their 'modern' acceptance of man's 'control' over Nature and his own Destiny. This world is symbolized in the action of the play by the traditional healing arts of Iya Agba and Iya Mata, arts which are defined by their wholeness and by their central concept of man as the vessel of power and not the creator of it.

When Bero questions them, significantly as intent on pinning down the 'name' (label) of their power as with As they make clear what the alternative source can be which has been lost by Madmen and Specialists alike in the modern world.

> BERO: By tomorrow I want you out.
> IYA AGBA: We want to help him.
> BERO: No one needs help from you. Now get out of my way.
> IYA AGBA: Maybe you do.
> BERO: Do I have to fling you aside!
> IYA AGBA [stands aside.]: Pass, then.
> [She lets him take a few steps, then.] Your sister owes us a debt.
> BERO: [stops, turns slowly]:
> If you know what is good for you, you will never let me hear that again.
> IYA AGBA: We took her into the fold – did she tell you that? To teach what we know, a pupil must come into the fold.
> BERO: What fold? Some filthy thieving cult?
> IYA AGBA: It's no light step for man or woman.
> BERO: And what ... cult is this?
> IYA AGBA: Not any cult you can destroy. We move as the Earth moves, nothing more. We age as Earth ages.
> BERO: But you're afraid to tell me the name.
> IYA AGBA: I try to keep fools from temptation.
> BERO [instantly angry.]: Watch it, old woman, your age earns no privileges with me.
> IYA AGBA: Nothing does from what we hear. So you want to know what cult, do you?
> BERO: I can ask your – pupil.
> [He turns round to go back to his house.]
> IYA AGBA: She won't tell you. Take it from me. She won't.
> [Bero stops without turning, waits.]

Your mind has run farther than the truth. I see it searching going round and round in darkness. Truth is always too simple for a desperate mind.
BERO [going.]. I shall find out.
IYA AGBA: Don't look for the sign of broken bodies or wandering souls. Don't look for the sound of fear or the smell of hate. Don't take a bloodhound with you; we don't mutilate bodies.
BERO: Don't teach me my business.
IYA AGBA: If you do, you may find him circle back to your door.
BERO: Watch your mouth old hag.
IYA AGBA: You want the name? But how much would it tell you, young man? We put back what we take, in one form or another. Or more than we take. It's the only law. What laws do you obey?
BERO: You are proscribed, whatever you are, you are banned.
IYA AGBA: What can that mean? You'll proscribe Earth itself? How does one do that?
BERO: I offer you a last chance.
IYA AGBA: The fool is still looking for names. How much would it tell you?
BERO: You'll find out when they come for you.
IYA AGBA: What will you step on young fool? Even on the road to damnation a man must rest his foot somewhere. [Bero marches furiously back to the surgery.] (pp. 58-9)

The figures of the two old women point the way to an alternative possible use of the destruction and pain caused by war and suffering. Viewed in the context of the whole culture it can be seen as a means to regeneration, a purgation or cleansing which can image forth man's rejection of the past and his acceptance of the need for new beginnings, different, yet founded in an acceptance of his wholeness through past, present and future.

The destruction visited on Madman and Specialist by the Old Women is the other side of the gift of past to present. The traditional wisdom offered to the present in the figure of Bero's sister, Si Bero, has been abused by father and brother. Now the alternative restorative of fire and pain must sweep away the abuse in a destructive image of the wholeness of all, a concept as expressible through the consumption of flesh (sacrifice) as through its nourishment (libation).

IYA AGBA: I waste no strength on carrion. I leave him to earth's rejection.
SI BERO: Give me more time. I have the power of a mother with him.
IYA MATA [gently.]: We waited as long as we could, daughter.
IYA AGBA: Time has run out. Do you think time favours us? Can I sleep easy when my head is gathering mould on your shelves?
SI BERO: You said yourself nothing goes to waste.
IYA AGBA: What is used for evil is also put to use. Have I not sat with the knowledge of abuse these many days and kept the eyes of mind open?
IYA MATA: It cannot wait, daughter. Evil hands soon find a use for the best of things.
SI BERO: Let it wait my mothers, let it wait.
IYA AGBA [angrily.]: Rain falls and seasons turn. Night comes and goes – do you think they wait for the likes of you? I warned you when we took you in the fold ...
SI BERO: I'll repay it all I promise ...
IYA AGBA: I said this gift is not one you gather in one hand. If your other hand is fouled the first withers also.
IYA MATA: This is how we met it. No one can change that.
SI BERO [clutching Iya Mata around the knees.]:

Not you too. You were never as hard as she.

IYA MATA: Nothing we can do, daughter, nothing but follow the way as we met it.

SI BERO: And the good that is here? Does that count for nothing?

IYA AGBA: We'll put that into the test. Let us see how it takes to fire.

SI BERO: Fire?

IYA AGBA: It is only the dying embers of an old woman's life. The dying embers of earth as we knew it. Is that anything to fear?

SI BERO: We laboured hard together.

IYA AGBA: So does the earth on which I stand. And on which your house stands, woman. If you want the droppings of rodents on your mat I can only look on. But my head still fills your room from wall to wall and dirty hands touch it ...

SI BERO: No, no, nobody but myself ...

IYA AGBA: I need to sleep in peace ... (pp. 74-5)

In the final action Madman and Specialist are united in a single visual image when the Old Man dons the coat of his son and prepares to exorcise the As-ness ('the tick of the heretic') of man through the techniques of the surgical torturer/interrogater. Both are exorcisable only in terms of the fire which reduces all men to their essential unity. The fire must consume all, good and bad alike.

OLD MAN: Stop him! Fire! Fire! Riot! Hot Line! Armageddon!
[As he shouts, the Old Man snatches the Surgeon's coat from where it is hanging, puts it on, dons cap, pulls on the gloves and picks up a scalpel.]

OLD MAN [at the top of his voice.] Bring him over here. [He dons mask.] Bring him over here. Lay him out. Stretch him flat. Strip him bare. Bare! Bare! Bare his soul! Light the stove!

[They heave him onto the table and hold him down while the Old Man rips the shirt open to bare the Cripple's chest. Bero rushes in and takes in the scene, raises his pistol and aims at the Old Man.]

OLD MAN: Let us taste just what makes a heretic tick. [He raises the scalpel in a motion for incision. Bero fires. The Old Man spins, falls face upwards on the table as the Cripple slides to the ground from under him. A momentary freeze on stage. Then Si Bero rushes from the Old Women towards the surgery. Instantly Iya Agba hurls the embers into the store and thick smoke belches out from the doorway gradually filling the stage. Both women walk calmly away as Si Bero reappears in the doorway of the surgery. The Mendicants turn to look at her, break gleefully into their favourite song. The Old Women walk past their hut, stop at the spot where the Mendicants were first seen and look back towards the surgery. The song stops in mid-word and the lights snap out simultaneously.]

Bi o ti wa
Ni yio se wa
Bi o ti wa
Ni yio se wa
Bi o ti wa l'atete ko.

THE END

And yet, although the action would seem to imply that only the Old Women are left this is not an image of total destructiveness. Just as at the end of *The Road* there is a route forward. The key to this lies in the time-structure of the action. The destruction brought by the old women at the end of the play is both actual and ritual (existing on both planes at once in terms of the symbols integrated in the re-enactment on stage), just as is Professor's death at the end of *The*

Road. Thus the fire at the end of the play is both an actual event at the end of the stage events, and also a ritual re-enactment of the war which is the informing image of the play. Thus viewed ritually the war can be shown to lead not only to the madness and cruelty, the blindness and destruction of its immediate consequence but also to a possible future perception of the wholeness of existence which can grow out of the suffering and consuming pain men have experienced. The war is what we have seen, and with the results we have seen because men have made it in the images we have seen destroyed. If they can re-integrate those images with the wider perceptions the modern mind has neglected and cast aside then perhaps they can create out of this experience that possibility of regeneration which Soyinka sees as the essential and only goal of art and life.

The importance and originality of Soyinka's achievement can hardly be overestimated. Although writers like Achebe have a finish and completeness which command attention, it is in the occasionally tortuous but always rewarding work of Soyinka that the future possibilities for English writing in Nigeria seem to me to be most clearly foreshadowed. His novels are as demanding and fascinating as the plays. *The Interpreters* (1965) and *Season of Anomy* (1973) show the same urgency and restlessness, the same refusal to accept existing forms, and the same intelligence in adapting them to their new contexts. If I have not discussed them here it is because the plays seemed to offer the best route into an account of Soyinka's achievement as I understand it, and not because they have less merit. Also, the last writer I want to examine, the Guyanese writer Wilson Harris, has worked almost exclusively within the novel form, and so offers a separate opportunity to show how a different genre can be changed and developed when exposed to the opportunities and difficulties of a non-English social context.

If selection has been a difficulty with Soyinka it is even more so with Harris, who has more than thirteen novels and prose collections to his credit. I have decided to limit the discussion to three novels which cover the early, middle and later periods of Harris's work: *Palace of the Peacock* (1960); *Ascent to Omai* (1970); and *Black Marsden* (1972).

Wilson Harris's novels are difficult and complex. But I believe they offer a reward which well repays the task of reading them. They are not only intricate and fascinating individual works, but also steps in a journey towards a radical re-working of the novel form. The sources of this impulse, as Harris himself has noted, lie in the inadequacy of the traditional genre to record the peculiar features of the Guyanese experience. But beyond this and mediated through it lies the problem of how the novel should change to accommodate the transformations in human society which the technological and scientific advances of the twentieth century have brought about. For Harris, these transformations are not merely mechanical. They involve not only a reworking of the surface patterns of society, but also a profound challenge to the human imagination to digest wholly new ways of perceiving the relationship between objective phenomena and subjective reactions.

There is no better account of the problem for the novelist in this age than that offered by Harris in his essay *Tradition and The West Indian Novel.*[6] In the opening pages of this brilliant and provocative essay he analyzes the failure of the traditional novel of manners to accommodate the kinds of contradictory sources of experience which make up the West Indian tradition, and, as he sees it, the twentieth century condition.

> The consolidation of character is, to a major extent, the preoccupation of most novelists who work in the twentieth century within the framework of the nineteenth-century novel. Indeed the nineteenth-century novel has exercised a very powerful influence on reader and writer alike in the contemporary world. And this is not surprising after all since the rise of the novel in its

conventional and historical mould coincides in Europe with states of society which were involved in consolidating their class and other vested interests. As a result 'character' in the novel rests more or less on the self-sufficient individual – on elements of 'persuasion' (a refined or liberal persuasion at best in the spirit of the philosopher Whitehead) rather than 'dialogue' or 'dialectic' in the profound and unpredictable sense of person which Martin Buber, for example, evokes.
[*Tradition and The West Indian Novel* pp. 28-9]

This tradition, Harris argues, has promoted a false rhetorical 'logic' in narratives which the novelist, 'conservative' or 'radical', persuades the reader to accept. It has prevented an imaginative and personal engagement with the contradictory and overlapping possibilities buried in any experience, and fostered an acceptance by writer and reader alike of 'self-conscious and fashionable moralities' which insist that the 'tension which emerges is the tension of individuals – great or small – on an accepted plane of society we are persuaded has an inevitable existence'. This 'conventional mould' of form has far-reaching consequences, not only for the novel, but for the role art plays in shaping the individual consciousness in those societies it depicts. Thus, although superficially asocial and apolitical, Harris's novels, and his critical writings, are a plea for a profound radicalization of human perception, a radicalization which seeks to pass beyond the superficial world of labels to a true root of consciousness. The acceptance of the 'novel of persuasion' involves the acceptance of a simplified selection in place of a full imaginative apprehension of a person or an event. The danger that Harris sees is that

... the novel which consolidates situations to depict protest or affirmation is consistent with most kinds of over-riding advertisement and persuasion upon the writer for him to make national and political and social simplifications of experience in the world at large today. (p. 30)

Such a view of the novel has not been fashionable with many of Harris's West Indian contemporaries. In the urgency they feel towards the task of articulating to their audiences an unbiased version of their past and a message of unity and hope for the future, they have been impatient of Harris's demands for a more far-reaching oversight of both past and present as the indispensable ground for any adequate attempt to influence the future. Though one may sympathize with this impatience, one cannot help feeling the force of Harris's contention that

> ... it is one of the most ironic things with West Indians of my generation that they may conceive of themselves in the most radical political light but their approach to art and literature is one which consolidates the most conventional and documentary techniques in the novel. (p. 44)

Certainly nobody could accuse Wilson Harris of consolidating conventional techniques. Throughout his writing career he has been engaged in a sustained and consistent exploration of alternatives in form, diction and subject matter. This experimenting drive is sustained by Harris's conviction that the novel must change radically if it is to continue to be a sensitive guide to human values and human action. In the 'novel of persuasion' events are selected to create a pattern through which the significant values of a narrative emerge. In Harris's fiction this linear logic is replaced by a freer exploratory technique. An event is viewed as a point in a continuum, a crossing place of all the latent possibilities of the past out of which it has grown, and a junction for all the possible future consequences which flow from it. Harris seems, sometimes, to see himself as a scientist whose material is the subjective imagination. Like an experimenter, he tries to remain open to all the possibilities in a character or an event rather than to impose a consistent narrative connection on them. The resulting structure treats each event as a possible manifestation rather than an absolute and unique occurrence. When and how these possibilities surface and become dominant in the fiction depends not on a principle of prior 'selection' but on the pre-logical connections which the writer first intuits and then demonstrates as truthful by their enriching effect on the reader's perception. Thus the individual 'character' or 'event' is not the ultimate object of investigation. The novel does not seek to flesh out a character by building a consistent and directed picture of his outside actions and his inner motivations; it does not, in Harris's phrase, seek to 'consolidate' the character; rather it searches for the pattern of impulses which meet and are made manifest in and through this human personality, and in whom they find 'fulfilment'. Harris sees the radical dislocation involved in the West Indian 'native' tradition as a compelling source for this view of human personality and experience, and for his view of fiction as a tool to liberate consciousness from the imaginative straitjacket of social form. The West Indies, as we saw George Lamming note, is the archetypal melting-pot of the colonial period. Here wave after wave of colonizers came and went, bringing with them every possible variety of enslaved and denigrated human being that the economic systems could create. And before and behind this colonial experience there remained the hidden presence of the successive pre-Columbian civilizations whose pitifully decimated ancestors still interweave with the descendants of the new conquerors and their slaves like a persistent and inerradicable memory. As Harris has said, 'What in my view is remarkable about the West Indian in depth is a sense of subtle links, the series of subtle and nebulous links which are latent within him, the latent ground of old and new personalities.' (p. 28) Thus the West Indian experience in itself, forces the novelist to reconsider the form which he has inherited, as he explores these overlapping layers of historical identity and cultural influence. Similarly, the landscape, which West Indian writers have so often felt to be bare of historical depth, is only bare if we assume that human consciousness is formed only by the overt social forces which shape our structures and institutions. Thus for Naipaul the West Indies has no history because it has no contemporary institutions which predate the mass importation of alien forms in the colonial period, the period which, superficially, has shaped the existing social pattern. For Harris, on the other hand, this very bareness is a sharp reminder that the ancient 'architectures' of the pre-Columbian consciousness are still alive in living personalities; that in countries like Guyana, cultural and economic patterns reflecting these 'dead' worlds still exist though buried beneath disguising modern forms. So,

> ... the very bareness of the West Indian world reveals the necessity to examine closely the starting point of human societies. The diminution of man is not entirely accomplished and a relationship between man and the paradoxes of his world becomes evident as a relationship which can still have momentous consequences. (p. 14)

Harris's concern for the past is never merely documentary. He does not seek only to *record* the values of the past but to *recover* them for the West Indian writer and his audience as an alternative informing source to the values of the present. It is the moment of change he seeks, in which old and new come together, realized in a person, and so transformed into action. The explanation he seeks is of what motivates us here and now, and the grammar he articulates is that of our present, made up in part though it is of the buried significances which word and symbol carry with them into that present.

> We live in a twilight situation which half-remembers, half-forgets. As such the language of consciousness has to literally rediscover and reinform itself in the face of accretions of accent and privilege, the burden of 'sacred' usage or one-sidedness. (p. 64)

It is in the struggle against this imposed 'one-sidedness' of language that Wilson Harris's narrative form has been shaped.

Wilson Harris has talked about the new novelist he

envisages as 'the kind of writer who sets out again and again across a certain territory of primordial but broken recollection in search of a community whose existence he begins to discern within capacities of unique fiction.' In statements like this we can see the feeling Harris shares with a writer like D.H. Lawrence that the novel has within it the possibility to become a uniquely effective tool for investigating the buried possibilities of human personality, a rigorous and incisive tool of insight into the human condition. At the beginning it is the growth of the human personality against his own Guyanese background to which he turns. In his early novels he explores the unique combination of geographical and cultural overlappings which shape the Guyanese experience, and which lie buried within the apparent structures of contemporary life. In the first of these, *Palace of the Peacock*,[7] both the general method and the purpose of Harris's fiction are clearly realized, and despite developments and a broadening of scene and incident in the later fiction these methods and purposes have remained consistent throughout his work.

The outline of the novel concerns a journey by outboard canoe up one of the fierce, turbulent rivers of Guyana. Beginning on the coastland, the journey traces a route through the interior, where the river cuts unscaleable gorges through the densly jungled savannah until it is stopped by the barrier of a waterfall on the 'escarpment' of the impenetrable interior. But, it quickly becomes apparent, that the voyage is less an actual event than a journey into the meaning of the Guyanese experience for narrator and reader. Yet, it seems to me that it is wrong to assume too completely that the narrative is not tied to an actual descriptive process. There is a quite clear distinction between allegory and the use of evocative imagery which lifts Harris's prose above the merely documentary. The heart of this experience is the complex history of Guyana, and the imprint of successive waves of influence on the face of this intractable landscape; and this experience is present in those who inhabit this world as a living reality, not just a symbolic memory. Thus Donne, the brutal and yet inspiring conquistador figure who captains the boat's 'crew'; the woman Mariella, the ideal of conquest he pursues; Carroll, the negro boy brought up and fostered by the Indian Vigilance; Vigilance himself; and the Portuguese mulattos, the da Silva twins, are all figures clearly and sensitively portrayed in a 'realistic' mode. Through each of them, however, we become aware, of a further strand of past which is woven into the pattern of the present action. The heart of Harris's insight is that this past is not lost, but is actively fulfilled in the human beings it has shaped and is shaping at this moment in time we choose to call the present. Thus, in the figure of Carroll, for example, there is a finely realized portrait of the curious eagerness of adolescence, with its over-readiness to identify itself with the feelings and pains of others, and a clear indication of the connection in his character between this personal characteristic and the residual patterns imposed by the historical suffering of the enslaved negro transportees.

> Schomburg spoke in an old man's querulous, almost fearful voice, ... 'How you feeling son?' he had turned and was addressing me. Carroll saw my difficulty and answered, 'Fine, fine,' he cried with a laugh. His voice was rich and musical and young. Schomburg grinned, seasoned, apologetic, a little unhappy, seeing through the rich boyish mask. Carroll trembled a little. I felt his work-hardened hands, so accustomed to making a tramp's bed in the bottom of a boat and upon the hard ground of the world's night. This toughness and strength and enduring sense of limb were a nervous bundle of longing. (p. 29)

Carroll here is not symbolically used to 'represent' the negro element in the Guyanese past; rather, it is this element of the past present in him which Wilson Harris seeks to expose, and to show functioning as one of the determinants actively at work in the formation of his personality and the role he plays in the novel.

The opening book establishes the basic structural pattern. This journey is in itself a re-enactment of all previous such attempts at penetrating to the central core, the meaning of this new world. In this sense, for the elusive 'I' figure it is a journey back into himself, since, as he perceives it, it re-enacts the history of the world which has brought them to this moment of experience. In his imagination this landscape they travel is a paradigm for his own person, symbolic of all the successive waves of influence which have fulfilled themselves in his personality.

> The map of the savannahs was a dream. The names Brazil and Guiana were colonial conventions I had known from childhood. I clung to them now as to a curious necessary stone and footing, even in my dream, the ground I knew I must not relinquish. They were an actual stage, a presence, however mythical they seemed to the universal and spiritual eye. They were as close to me as my ribs, the rivers and the flatlands, the mountains and heartland I intimately saw. I could not help cherishing my symbolic map, and my bodily prejudice like a well-known room and house of superstition within which I dwelt. I saw this kingdom of man turned into a colony and battleground of spirit, a priceless tempting jewel I dreamed I possessed. (p. 20)

Harris has warned readers of the danger of fastening too readily on 'ideas' and neglecting the flow of narrative in which they are fixed.

> I believe it is necessary to study the text and texture of novels closely. It is easy to make propaganda of ideas, to overlook actual texts, to lose both the pleasure and profit involved in sensing the authenticity of narrative as the active medium of ideas.[8]

The passage I have quoted may serve as an example. Read in isolation it may be seen as a positive, even celebratory description of the essential, central relationship between the narrator and the Guyanese landscape. But viewed in the overall context of the developing narrative it is revealed as a response which the narrator has to slough off if he is to come to a true understanding of himself and of the world he inhabits. From this 'bodily prejudice' he is liberated into a more complete accord with the vision of his 'spiritual eye' when, lost in the forest a few pages later, he becomes aware that this identification of his own consciousness with the reality around him is the result of the social conventions ('superstitions') through which his perception of this reality is strained. When he is lost in the primordial forest, and so is 'liberated' from the symbolic map of his contemporary superstitions, he perceives the latent events and personalities beneath the conventional maps of Guyana and of himself; the skeletons of himself and his culture which he must 'lose' himself to re-discover.

> The carpet on which I stood had an uncertain place within splintered and timeless roots whose fibre was stone in the tremulous ground. I lowered my head a little, blind almost, and began forcing a new path into the trees away from the river's opening and side.
>
> A brittle moss and carpet appeared underfoot, a dry pond and stream whose course and reflection and image had been stamped for ever like the breathless outline of a dreaming skeleton in the earth ... The forest rustled and rippled with a sigh and ubiquitous step. I stopped dead where I was, frightened for no reason whatever. The step near me stopped and stood still. I stared around me wildly, in surprise, and terror, and my body grew faint and trembling as a woman's or a child's. I gave a loud ambushed cry which was no more than an echo of myself – a breaking and grotesque voice, man and boy, age and youth speaking together.
>
> (*Palace of the Peacock* pp. 27-8)

Through this experience of the hidden depths of the world about him, depths not charted on his contemporary symbolic map, he is brought into touch with the hidden depths in himself. The process is like that we encounter in Romantic poetry (the Wordsworthian echo in the passage quoted above is surely no coincidence), especially in Coleridge, a poet whom Harris sees as very much at the beginning of the imaginative process he has inherited.[9] Coleridge would certainly have understood the experiences which Harris has referred to as the discovery of catalysts of experience within the density of space

> ... so deep imprest
> Sink the sweet scenes of childhood, that mine eyes
> I never shut amid the sunny ray,
> But straight with all their tints thy waters rise,
> Thy crossing plank, thy marge with willows grey,
> And bedded sand that vein'd with various dyes
> Gleams through thy bright transparence!
> (Coleridge *Sonnet: To the River Otter*)

The crossing plank here is a perfect example of such a catalyst, an object or a moment of experience through which the person in the present may suddenly become aware of himself as both the inheritor and the creator of the past which flows through him.

After the brief pause at the Mariella Mission the voyage resumes, the crew having cast off the last links with the immediate present by their decision to venture beyond the bounds of the possible, since the river above the mission is profoundly threatening at this time of year and dangerous. One by one the crew of the vessel are drowned or killed as, guided by the ancient Arawak woman whom Donne has 'subdued' they journey up the river to the falls near Sorrow Hill where the names of an earlier crew are inscribed. This crew's names match those of Donne and his men, as of course they must, since in this experience (Guyana) the past must be alive in all present ventures under the particular guises handed down by the flow of time: Portuguese half-breed; Elizabethan conquistadore; nervous, overstung negro slave;

placid, half-dreaming Indian, and so forth. In Book 3, The Second Death, the historical process is re-enacted as one by one the living waves of men who have sought to subdue the land perish again. For the narrator the journey is growing more and more to be one which he views with his 'spiritual eye', and as each man dies so he is forced to cast off one more protective layer of historical illusion and recognize his complicity and partnership in the experience which they have represented. When at last they arrive at the falls beyond which their voyage cannot proceed they have passed beyond the driving force of personality, even that of the abstract 'incalculable devouring principle' of the ego-centred Donne to a place where 'Water start dream, rock and stone start dream, tree trunk and tree root dreaming, bird and beast dreaming.' They have arrived at the place where ideas and objects are one, a time when history has not yet begun.

Here, as in the Dreamtime of the Australian aboriginal, action is indivisible from idea, and the distinction of animate and inanimate is washed out in a universal and overwhelming impulse to become, an impulse out of which all forms are shaped and all purposes wrought to the end of time.

The final section, Paling of Ancestors, is the culmination of the voyage and also the return, for the voyage turns away now from the ceaseless, goal-orientated voyage into the heartland and becomes a vertical struggle up the face of the immaculate waterfall towards the only escape possible. Any single reading of this complex novel must be offered tentatively, but it seems to me, at least, that here we witness the struggle against the logic of history (the struggle back against the tide of events) and the realization that the only route is through the transcendental, through a vision that can encompass the whole length of time (the river) in a single, continuous plane (the waterfall). Here we enter a world which is bathed in that visionary light which haunts the imagination of man from the beginning of time ('the light that never was on sea or land'),

Right and left grew the universal wall of cliff they knew,

and before them the highest waterfall they had ever seen moved and still stood upon the escarpment. They were plainly astonished at the immaculate bridal veil falling motionlessly from the river's tall brink. The cliffs appeared to box and imprison the waterfall. A light curious fern grew out of the stone, and pearls were burning and smoking from the greenest brightest dwarfs and trees they remembered. (p. 29)

The waterfall is a 'paling' (a fence) which shuts off the flow of ancestry by containing it. Within the force of the waterfall all the sources of the river are momentarily contained and mixed. Thus, as they struggle up its face they see in the turbulent mist and spray windows into the past of man, symbols of the great universal impulses which from age to age are reflected in individual lives: sacrifice (the window of the carpenter where a Christ figure works with the very tools which will eventually nail him to the cross); madonna and child, (the universal source of comfort and betrayal, mercy and sternness), the hunted beast (prehistoric image of the self-same sacrifice, side-pierced by the same spear, that modern man has worshipped). Image upon image, each sustaining in its own reflection the same continuing universal impulse. Through the waterfall the narrator gazes into the void from which all structures ('sacred' images) come, and to which all return in a perennial process of flow from past to future and future to past.

They were a ghost of light and that was all. The void of themselves alone was real and structural. All else was dream borrowing its light from a dark invisible source akin to human blindness and imagination that looked through nothingness all the time to the spirit that secured life. (p. 141)

The image of the peacock, whose palace is created in the blending of spirit with spirit, symbolized by the waterfall, is an image of this underpinning force which, once perceived, holds the contradictory experiences of life together.

> It was the dance of all fulfilment I now held and knew deeply, cancelling my forgotten fear of strangeness and catastrophe in a destitute world.
>
> This was the inner music and voice of the peacock ... Each of us now held at last in his arms what he had been seeking and what he had eternally possessed. (p. 152)

In this recognition the narrator is reconciled to the meaning of the past in the moment that he fully perceives it as an active future force within himself, subject to alteration just as much and just as little as he himself is, the vessel which, in this present moment, gives it shape and consciousness.

Palace of the Peacock is the most consciously 'poetic' of Harris's fictions, and has been compared with a quarry whose many rich veins are the obsessive themes which the later novels continue to mine. Certainly the idiosyncratic patterns of Harris's novels are cumulative, and a full study of his work would involve an appreciation of the way in which central images develop in force and resonance as they re-appear in book after book e.g. scarecrow or dreaming eye; clown; theatre; skeleton etc ... The strong preoccupation with the Guyanese landscape and with the symbolic correspondence he draws between its physical features and the human personalities who inhabit it continues unabated through his first four novels: *Palace of the Peacock* (1960); *The Far Journey of Oudin* (1961); *The Whole Armour* (1962); and *The Secret Ladder* (1963). Although this theme is also present in the later work, for example in *Heartland* (1964) and in certain aspects of *Tumatumari* (1968) there seems to be a gradual deepening of interest in the world of personal relationships and family structures in the novels of the late sixties, *The Waiting Room*, for example. This process goes hand in hand with the strengthening of the role of the central narrator, an inward-turning rhetoric which frequently employs recollection, memoir or even diary form, and an increasingly self-conscious examination of the structures employed as they are turned in upon themselves by the narrative consciousness. *Ascent to Omai* (1973)[10] seems to me to be the culminating example of this gradual shift in emphasis over the decade of the sixties. *Ascent to Omai* is cast in the form of a trial or investigation, an enquiry on the part of the protagonist, Victor, into the events and forces which have shaped his present. But, at the same time it seems to be an investigation into the validity of the narrative form it employs. At moments the novel seems to be a demonstration of the techniques it employs, and to verge on a defence of the purpose and means of Harris's own special theory of fiction. It is the interweaving of this overt narrative purpose with what one might see as a critical defence of its techniques that makes the novel especially useful as a way into an understanding of Harris's writings.

As in *Palace of the Peacock* the parallels between the historical span of time and its individual correlations within the novel are carefully pointed. The narrative centres on Victor, the son of Adam, the violent dispossessed welder who burns down the factory at which he works. This story is shown to be representative as well as unique, to contain within itself the essential shape of the giant historical and social forces which have helped to form modern Guyana. But it is part of Harris's thesis that these forces can only be effectively understood when mediated through such an individual narrative. To try and comprehend them divorced from the complex and contradictory residue which only the individual instance can fully reveal is to oversimplify and distort. The argument for the living witness of the individual to the forces which pass through him is presented in the novel in the form of a poem which the father, Adam, has apparently written – though, of course, it is in fact a manifestation of Victor's mind not Adam's, since everything that occurs within the novel is contained within the 'imagination' of the narrator Victor, whose reveries form the central narrative point of view. This poem, Fetish, is a miniature symbol of the purpose of the novel as a whole, since it seeks to present the experience of Adam in its contradictory and fractured wholeness rather than in a tidily organized pattern imposed on it from without. The prosecuting counsel who, one suspects, is in part representative of some of Harris's own critics, attacks the view of history represented by Fetish as

> All that exotic pseudo-historical rubbish ... I know the sort of splintered world – neither capitalist nor communist. The museum of man. Left Bank manifesto stuff ... Overplayed guitar in the middle of nowhere, it's so uninspiring, so weak in this day and age ...
> (*Ascent to Omai* p. 72)

The defence counsel's answer might well be Harris's own.

> Yes, indeed what a mess. But mess – rubbish – is invaluable. It is, in fact, a new experimental source of wealth. Everything depends on whether you are serious about it or cynical about it. If you're serious you won't just sweep it under the carpet and invest, after that, in a number of tidy self-indulgent rationalizations which ignore the light of the future. Fetish seeks to break this *tidiness* because, in fact, it's all part of a callous or callouses of conceit we plaster upon everything. You and I appear to agree about this. As Dr. Wall will tell you – and his interest in Fetish is less in the poem than in the borderline depressive state of Adam (buried, no doubt, as you rightly imply in left bank manifestos and museums of man, exotic rubbish heaps and reservations) – as Dr. Wall will tell you, I repeat, what Adam is trying to salvage or uncover is a sacramental vacancy within the flotsam and jetsam of a collective experience that has oppressed him and continues to oppress him in the name of a puritanical humanity, whereas it may well be the fuel of a compassionate divinity ...
> (*Ascent to Omai* pp. 72-3)

Here, as elsewhere in Harris's writings, we are impressed with the seriousness and urgency which he brings to his idea of the novel's purpose. It is a tool for recovery and for the establishment through this recovery of a truly effective perspective on man's place in the world. The events of the novel are unified through one act, that of the imagination. Everything that occurs is Victor's act of imagining the events and peoples of his own past as living presences in his own personality. The Ascent to Omai is an ascent out of his own immediate personality into a liberation from the ego, from that 'monolithic name' by which we define our identity, and which buries all the latent personalities which shape our surfaces unawares. The form of the novel must change to be able to express this real form of history. Its concept of character in time must develop to accommodate our awareness of the many layers of reality, past and present, which make up an instant of experience.

> The judge shuffled his pack: Jack of trades, scavenger and sovereign of spirits, housecoat of stars, breadwinner of suns. He was suddenly stricken by a sense of 'emptiness' as though the characters he attacked or defended, also attacked him *in his own monolithic name*, defended him blindly as compassionate alien within mandala or fortress. They were as much his disabled creation as he theirs – all roles were interchangeable – judge, judged, victor, victim, Adam etc., etc. as parts of a broken translation and legacy of history.
>
> They and he constituted a spectral host advancing from a citadel or form to the same blinding citadel, misconception or form (p. 83)

It is this citadel of form which must be stormed and taken age after age.

> The Judge shuffled his cards with a sigh. He wanted, he knew, to write a kind of novel or novel history in which the spectre of time was the main character, and the art of narrative the obsessed ground/lighthouse of security/insecurity. (p. 83)

The key to the task is the rejection of time as an orderly, linear process in which significances are trapped in an inexorable order. Such a form fossilizes our awareness of ourselves and our growth into a museum exhibit. Past, present and future become permanently frozen, isolated, strata, shut off from one another. It is essential to recover our awareness of time as a spiritual dimension whose flow cannot be trapped within the spatial periods of form. Language must be freed from a grammar which preaches a falsely lucid organization of experience.

> This obsession with time as comma and period, age and full-stop, was, in his view, something that sprang from a base idolatry, from a desire to conscript time itself into a material commodity. (p. 84)

But time is not a material object that can be traded, bought or renewed by a repetitive ritual or sacrifice on the altered form. For Harris, as *Ascent to Omai* makes clear, the traditional novel is as sterile as the Aztec human sacrifice. Time, the world, reality, cannot be restored by the ritual disembowelling of an experience which we call 'art', turning human lives into a 'fortress or factory of time'. Instead what we have to seek is 'a qualitative illumination' in place of a 'quantitative bank of time'. The novelist needs to see

> into the unique density and transparency of his victim (spectral character and dust) and [refrain] therefore from inflicting a senseless ordeal on what was in essence the ghost of the universe, serial participation in time, universal subsistence of memory, mature void ... (p. 85)

Harris is quite aware of the reception this is likely to provoke, and in the judge's reverie we can, perhaps, hear echoes of Harris's own preoccupation and belief.

> He pulled a card from his pack. PROPHET had been written there. Yes – the judge sighed – he would be accused of being vatic. How could he begin to explain to the ignorant and impatient that *time*, year and day, was

involved in his prophecies as a spectral function within which like/unlike – the ruined fortress of personality – could subsist *now* as *then* (today or a thousand years hence) as *blank* cheque of compassion rather than bankrupt materialism or passion? As a consciousness without content which nonetheless permitted all alien contents to exist: as stigmata of the void equivalent to the frailest felt cross of humanity, the wine of sacrifice, acute needle, perilous sensation, depths of healing, abyss of humility rather than over-stimulation, uniform prejudice, callous throne, heights of the banal. (p. 85)

The rest of the novel which follows this statement is a reworking of the material assembled up until this point, involving a fascinating internalization of the 'narrative' point of view. The novel we have read now becomes the novel the judge is writing, and the pack of events is reshuffled to permit the reader to view the same events from a new perspective.

'Do you remember?' the judge addressed the hidden *personae* in his pack, blurred masks or readers looking over his shoulder backwards from the future: flicked the pages of his book like an expert gambler with currencies of time – obverse and reverse. On one side *judge* on the other *judged*. On one side again *father* on the other *son*. On one side still again *ancient* on the other *modern*. (p. 86)

The richness of *Ascent to Omai* and its highly self-conscious probings of its own form has a quality of desperation about it. Perhaps this reflects Harris's sense at the time that his work, although always eliciting respectful noises from the reviewers, was not really communicating the essential truths as he saw them about art and the vital role the artistic imagination had to play in restoring a sense of wholeness to our experience of life, past and present. Certainly, there seems to be a kind of momentary defeat suffered by Victor when he declares

Time to shut up. This was his last novel. If he lived for

another hour, day, year, century – in his flight to OH
MY – *these pages must serve as his epitaph.* (p. 124)

But despite such misgivings the novel ends on a note of hope, as Victor finds 'on the horizon of dreams' the integrative vision which permits him to see in the ruined fragments of personality which constitute his father and his memory of him the 'godhead in the man; the man in the godhead'. Here, perhaps, more than in any other Harris novel we find the most succinct definition of the role he sees the imagination has to play in human affairs, and the credo he professes as artist and man.

It was not his object to exploit his material within a monolithic cast or mould, sentiment or callous, enchantment or substitute. These exploitations were better left to intellectuals – and he was not an intellectual in any given predictable fashion or creed. He was a creative struggler who, in the actual task of being born through words, *saw* – as upon a strange land of primordial/broken vessels – signposts he had either forgotten or had never seen before.

In this respect the struggle was also a voyage – a real sometimes inextricably woven series of adventures, painful and horrifying. But always profoundly true, profoundly necessary since it was a quest for authentic correspondences with the chained soul, the soul of the child, the silent portrait on the wall he had once been long long ago. (pp. 123-4)

Ascent to Omai seems to represent a crisis point and a renewal in Harris's work. When he returns to writing full-length novels after a period in which he concentrated on other forms, notably his reworking of pre-Columbian, traditional myths he expands his horizons geographically, and ventures on his first novel set outside Guyana. For Harris, as he makes clear in comments elsewhere,[11] this step was an important one, as it represents the moment when he is able to perceive through an alternative landscape and mythos one of those 'catalysts of experience within the density of space' in a culture other than that of his childhood. The resulting novel, *Black Marsden*, set in Edinburgh, the home of Harris's Scots wife, may symbolize his stretching out to build into his fiction the accumulated experiences of his adult life, as his earlier novels have drawn on the shapes and patterns of his childhood world. The same process is clearly at work in his latest novel *Companions of the Day and Night* (1975), which is set in Mexico and which develops the diary form of narration which features in *Ascent to Omai* and, more centrally, in *Black Marsden*.[12] Ironically labelled, 'tabula rasa' comedies, a concept which for Harris must sum up the limitations inherent in the impoverished logical forms of the eighteenth and nineteenth centuries,[13] these novels explore the process of creation and destruction implicit in the division of the world into dominant and subdued cultures, rich and poor, black and white, technologically-rich and materially-poor. As one would expect, Harris's view of the process is not a simple one. For him ruler and ruled, conqueror and conquered are involved in a shared process, a process of mutual erosion. In *Black Marsden*, through the figure of Goodrich, he explores the terrible price paid by modern man for his inheritance of a

> civilization that had left its impress in almost every crook and cranny of the known world. A civilization that had been showered with gifts, resources, materials beyond the wildest dreams of societies in earlier centuries. A civilization therefore which invited a kind of disaster (as with every bridegroom of fate wedded to universal resources), a kind of backlash from those cultures which had given all they possessed, and from 'nature' which had been drained of so much ...
> (*Black Marsden* p. 104)

But he is less concerned to affix guilt than to explore the hidden shaping processes worked by this experience on exploiter and exploited alike, to observe the hypnotic fascination which the enigmatic Black Marsden exerts on the depleted Goodrich, and to assert the continuity and continual renewal implicit even in the most destructive and desolate periods of the human experience. At the end of the novel the terminology of victory and defeat seem to be exhausted as universals. Freeing himself by an effort of will from the draining force of Marsden, Goodrich is able to assert the role he can play as a manifestation of an 'eternal apparition of spirit, however denuded, however misted over, however solitary, however wedded to time and place.' But, although 'armed by a strange inner tide of decision, a strange fire of secret resolution, he felt alone, utterly alone, as upon a post-hypnotic threshold at the heart of one of the oldest cities in Europe.' The process of waking from such a long and deep hypnotic spell, the spell which has laid itself over the European consciousness for long centuries, blocking out its roots to the 'world's night' from which it and all other consciousness springs, will be a long and difficult one. Goodrich, at the end of the novel, is left, typically for Harris, on the threshold of hope, but firmly within a continually changing future in which nothing is ever changed and everything is always changing.

It is, perhaps, appropriate to end this brief survey of the new African and West Indian writing in English with this account of two writers whose careers are characterized by a vigorous drive to explore the unique possibilities of their position as non-English writers using English. Whatever happens in the future, and whether or not the urge to use this unexpected legacy continues their achievements and those of their contemporaries have already made it impossible for those of us who share this language to ignore the ways in which they have changed our perception of the world in which we live.

SECTION 5—NOTES

1 E.g. Kofi Awoonor 'Voyager and the Earth' *New Letters*; Univ. of Missouri-Kansas City; Vol 40; No. 1; Autumn, 1973; pp. 88-89.
2 Though this point can be overstressed as was pointed out to me recently by Dapo Adelugba of Ibadan Theatre Arts Department in Nigeria. Certain traditional Nigerian drama does exist with a defined audience/performer separation and a linear narrative/celebratory form e.g. in the court entertainment traditions of the Yoruba.
3 MORELL, Karen L. (ed.), *In Person: Achebe, Awoonor, and Soyinka*; African Studies Programme; Institute for Comparative and Foreign Area Studies; Univ. of Washington; Seattle, 1975; pp. 94-5.
4 SOYINKA, Wole, *The Road*; Three Crowns; Oxford U.P., 1965; pp. 18-19.
5 SOYINKA, Wole, *Madmen and Specialists*; Methuen; London, 1971; p. 271.
6 In Wilson Harris, *Tradition, the Writer and Society – Critical Essays*; New Beacon Books; London, 1967; pp. 28-48.
7 Wilson Harris, *Palace of the Peacock*; Faber; London, 1960.
8 HARRIS, Wilson 'A Talk on the Subjective Imagination' *New Letters*; University of Missouri-Kansas City; Vol. 40, No. 1; Autumn, 1973; p. 45.
9 HARRIS, Wilson 'A Talk on the Subjective Imagination' p. 42. 'One would have to turn to Melville to sense the beginnings of this kind of thing in the novel, to a poet like Coleridge, or a novelist like Conrad'.
10 HARRIS, Wilson, *Ascent to Omai*; Faber; London, 1970.
11 HARRIS, Wilson 'A Talk on the Subjective Imagination' in *New Letters*; pp. 47-58.
12 HARRIS, Wilson, *Black Marsden*; Faber; London, 1972.
13 The more positive connotations of the term are hinted at in the essay in *New Letters*.

BIBLIOGRAPHY

The bibliography cannot hope to be exhaustive. It seeks to give readers information on the works of the main writers discussed in the text so that they can follow up their development for themselves. In addition it suggests some sources for general critical reading, and some basic bibliographical tools in this area. Please note: I have not included all articles or books mentioned in the text unless they seem relevant to the limited purposes of this general bibliography. Details of these are usually included in the relevant footnotes.

WRITERS

ACHEBE, Chinua (Nigeria)

Things Fall Apart; Heinemann Educ.; London, 1958.
No Longer at Ease; Heinemann Educ.; London, 1960.
Arrow of God; Heinemann Educ.; London, 1964.
A Man of the People; Heinemann Educ.; London, 1966.
Chike and the River (Children's story) Cambridge U.P.; Camb., 1966.
Beware, Soul Brother; Heinemann Educ.; London, 1972. (poems)
    Reissued with additional poems in America as:
Christmas in Biafra; Doubleday; New York, 1973.
Girls at War (stories); Heinemann Educ.; London, 1972.
How the Leopard Got His Claws (children's story); with John Iroaganadu; Rex Collings; London, 1973.
Morning Yet on Creation Day; Heinemann Educ.; London, 1975.

AMADI, Elechi (Nigeria)

The Concubine; Heinemann Educ.; London, 1966.
The Great Ponds; Heinemann Educ.; London, 1969.
Isiburu (play); Heinemann Educ.; London, 1973.
Sunset in Biafra (war memoir); Heinemann Educ.; London, 1973.

BIBLIOGRAPHY

ANTHONY, Michael (Trinidad)

The Games Were Coming; Andre Deutsch; London, 1963.
The Year in San Fernando; André Deutsch; London, 1965; reissued Heinemann Educ.; Caribbean Writer's Series; London, 1970.
Green Days By the River; Deutsch; London, 1965; reissued Heinemann Educ.; Caribbean Writers Series; London, 1973.
Cricket In the Road and other stories; André Deutsch; London, 1973; reissued Heinemann Educ.; Caribbean Writer's Series; London, 1973.
King of the Masquerade; Nelson; London, 1973.
David Frost Introduces Trinidad and Tobago; Dent; London, 1973. (ed.)
Profile Trinidad: a Historical Survey from the Discovery to 1900; Macmillan; London, 1975.

ARMAH, Ayi Kwei (Ghana)

The Beautyful Ones Are Not Yet Born; Heinemann Educ.; London, 1969.
Fragments; Houghton Mifflin; Boston, 1970.
Why Are We So Blest?; Doubleday; New York, 1972.

AWOONOR, Kofi (George Awoonor-Williams) – (Ghana)

Rediscover and other poems; Mbari Pubs.; Ibadan, 1964.
Messages – poems from Ghana (edited with G. Adali-Mortty); Heinemann Educ.; London, 1970.
Night of My Blood (poems); Doubleday; New York, 1971.
This Earth, My Brother ... (novel); Heinemann Educ.; London, 1971.
Ride Me, Memory; Greenfield Review Press; New York, 1973.
Guardians of the Sacred Word; Traditional African Literature Series; NOK Pubs.; New York, 1974.
The Breast of the Earth: a Survey of the History, Culture and Literature of Africa, South of the Sahara; Doubleday; New York, 1974.
Where is the Missisippi Panorama? 1974.

HARRIS, Wilson (Guyana)

Eternity to Season; Georgetown; British Guiana (Guyana); 1954. (poems)
Palace of the Peacock; Faber; London, 1960.
The Far Journey of Oudin; Faber; London, 1961.
The Whole Armour; Faber; London, 1962.
The Secret Ladder; Faber; London, 1963.
Heartland; Faber; London, 1964.
The Eye of the Scarecrow; Faber; London, 1965.
The Waiting Room; Faber; London, 1967.
Tumatumari; Faber; London, 1968.
Ascent to Omai; Faber; London, 1970.
The Sleepers of Roraima – a Carib Trilogy; Faber; London, 1970.

The Age of the Rainmakers; Faber; London, 1971.
Black Marsden; Faber; London, 1972.
Companions of the Day and Night; Faber; London, 1975.
Tradition, the Writer and Society (Collected essays); New Beacon Books; London, 1967.
The Whole Armour and The Secret Ladder (reissued as a single volume) Faber; London, 1967.
Genesis of the Clowns; Faber; To be published shortly at time of compilation.

LAMMING, George *(Barbados)*

In the Castle of My Skin; Michael Joseph; London, 1953; reissued by Longmans, 1970.
The Emigrants; Michael Joseph; London, 1954.
Of Age and Innocence; Michael Joseph; London, 1958.
Season of Adventure; Michael Joseph; London, 1960.
The Pleasures of Exile (non-fiction); Michael Joseph; London, 1960.
Natives of My Person; Longmans Caribbean; Port o' Spain, 1972; reissued by Pan (Picador Books); London, 1974.
Water With Berries; Longmans Caribbean; Port o' Spain, 1974.
Cannon Shots and Glass Beads: Modern black writing; (edited); Pan (Picador Books); London, 1974.

MAIS, Roger *(Jamaica)*

And most of all man; Jamaica City Printery: Kingston, 194-.
Face and other stories; Universal Printery; Kingston, 194-.
The Hills Were All Joyful Together; Jonathan Cape; London, 1953.
Brother Man; Jonathan Cape; London, 1954.
Black Lightning; Jonathan Cape; London, 1955.
The Hills Were etc., Brother Man and *Black Lightning* – reissued in one volume as *The Three Novels of Roger Mais*; Jonathan Cape; London, 1966; reprinted 1970.
Brother Man; Reissued as Caribbean Writers Series No. 10; Heinemann Educ.; London.

NAIPAUL, V.S. *(Trinidad)*

The Mystic Masseur; Deutsch; London, 1957; Penguin, London, 1964.
The Suffrage of Elvira; Deutsch; London, 1958; Penguin; London, 1969.
Miguel Street; Deutsch; London, 1959; Penguin; London, 1971.
A House for Mr. Biswas; Deutsch; London, 1961; Penguin; London, 1969.
The Middle Passage – the Caribbean Revisited (travel documentary); Deutsch; London, 1962; Penguin; London, 1969.
Mr. Stone and the Knights Companion; Deutsch; London, 1963; Four Square; London, 1966.

An Area of Darkness (travel documentary); Deutsch; London, 1964; Penguin; London, 1968.
The Mimic Men; Deutsch; London; 1967; Penguin; London, 1969.
A Flag on the Island (stories); Deutsch; London; 1967; Penguin; London, 1969.
The Loss of El Dorado (history); Deutsch; London, 1969.
In a Free State (novellas and travel fragments); Deutsch; London, 1971.
The Overcrowded Barracoon (essays and reviews); Deutsch; London, 1972.
Guerrillas; Deutsch; London, 1975.

NGUGI, Wa Thiong'o *(James Ngugi) (Kenya)*

Weep Not, Child; Heinemann Educ.; London, 1964.
The River Between; Heinemann Educ.; London, 1965.
A Grain of Wheat; Heinemann Educ.; London, 1967.
The Black Hermit (play); Heinemann Educ.; London, 1968.
Homecoming (essays); Heinemann Educ.; London, 1972.
Secret Lives (stories); Heinemann Educ.; London, 1974.
Petals of Blood (novel); Heinemann Educ; London, 1977.

OKIGBO, Christopher *(Nigeria)*

Labyrinths – poems; Heinemann Educ.; London, 1971.
In this collected edition of his poems the author states that 'Although these poems were written and published separately they are in fact, organically related' and adds that "The versions here preserved are, however, somewhat different and are final'.
   The various poem sequences first appeared in the following places,
Heavensgate; Mbari; Ibadan, 1962.
Silences; Part One in 'Transition' No. 8, 1963; Part Two published by Mbari; Ibadan, 1965.
Limits; Mbari; Ibadan, 1964.
Distances; in 'Transition' No. 16, 1964.
Path of Thunder – poems prophesying war; in Black Orpheus, February, 1968.
   All are reproduced in the collection *Labyrinths.*

REID, V.S. *(Jamaica)*

New Day; Alfred A. Knopf; New York, 1949; reissued Heinemann Educ.; Caribbean Writers Series No. 4; London, 1973.
The Leopard; Heinemann; London, 1958.
Sixty five; Blue Mountain Library; Longmans; London, 1960.
Young Warriors; Blue Mountain Library; Longmans, 1967.

SALKEY, Andrew *(Jamaica)*

A Quality of Violence; New Authors Ltd.; London, 1959.

Escape to an Autumn Pavement; Hutchinson; London, 1960.
(ed.) *Stories from the Caribbean;* Elek; London, 1965.
Earthquake (children's novel); Oxford U.P.; Oxford, 1965.
Hurricane; (children's novel); Oxford U.P.; Oxford, 1964.
Drought (children's novel); Oxford U.P.; Oxford, 1966.
Shark Hunters (children's novel); Nelson; London, 1966.
(ed.) *Caribbean Prose;* Evans Bros.; London, 1967.
(ed.) *West Indian Stories*; Faber; London, 1968.
The Late Emancipation of Jerry Stoker; Hutchinson; London, 1968.
The Adventures of Catullus Kelly; Hutchinson; London, 1969.
Jonah Simpson; Oxford U.P.; Oxford, 1969.
(ed.) *Breaklight; An anthology of Caribbean Poetry;* Hamish Hamilton; London, 1971.
Havana Journal; Penguin; Pelican Original; London, 1971.
Georgetown Journal; New Beacon Books; London, 1972.
Caribbean Essays; Evans Bros.; London, 1973.
Riot (children's novel); Oxford U.P.; Oxford, 1973.
Jamaica; Hutchinson; London, 1973.
(ed.) *Island voices; stories from the W. Indies*; Liveright; N.Y.; 1970.
Anancy's Score; Bogle-l'Ouverture Pubns.; 1973.

The two early novels, *A Quality of Violence* and *Escape to an Autumn Pavement* have been reprinted by Kraus Reprints; Black Experience Series No. 1; New York; 1970.

SELVON, Samuel (Trinidad)

An Island is a World; Wingate; London, 1955.
The Lonely Londoners; Wingate; London, 1956. Longman Caribbean, 1972.
Ways of Sunlight; MacGibbon and Kee; 1957; Longman Caribbean, 1973.
Turn Again Tiger; MacGibbon and Kee; London, 1958.
I Hear Thunder; MacGibbon and Kee; London, 1963.
The Housing Lark; MacGibbon and Kee; London, 1965.
A Drink of Water (children's story); Nelson; London, 1968.
The Plains of Caroni; MacGibbon and Kee; London, 1970.
Those Who Eat The Cascadura; Davis-Poynter; London, 1972.
Moses Ascending; Davis-Poynter; London, 1975.

SOYINKA, Wole (Nigeria)

The Lion and the Jewel (play); Three Crowns; OUP; Oxford, 1959.
The Swamp Dwellers; (1959); *The Trials of Brother Jero* (1961) and *The Strong Breed* (1962) in *Three Plays*; Three Crowns; OUP, 1969.
A Dance of the Forests (play) Three Crowns; OUP; Oxford, 1960.
The Road (play); Three Crowns; OUP; Oxford, 1964.
Kongi's Harvest (play); Three Crowns; OUP; Oxford, 1965.

The Interpreters (novel); Deutsch; London, 1964.
The Forest of a Thousand Daemons (trans. of D.O. Fagunwa's 'Ogboju ode ninu Igbo Irunmale'); Nelson; London, 1968.
Idanre and other Poems; Methuen; London, 1967.
Madmen and Specialists (play); Methuen; London, 1971.
Before the Blackout (Satirical Revue); Orisun Acting Editions; Ibadan, 1971.
A Shuttle in the Crypt; Hill & Wang, New York; 1972; London, 1972.
Poems from Prison; Rex Collings; London, 1969.
The Man Died (prison memoir); Rex Collings; London, 1972.
Jero's Metamorphosis; Methuen; London, 1973.
Camwood on the Leaves (play scripts); Methuen; London, 1973.
Season of Anomy (novel); Rex Collings; London, 1973.
The Bacchae (trans. from Euripides); Methuen; London, 1973.
(ed.) *Poems of Black Africa*, with introduction; Secker and Warburg; London, 1975; reissued in Heinemann African Writers Series; London, 1975.
Collected Plays 2 Vols.; Oxford University Paperbacks; Oxford, 1974.
The Interpreters (1964) has been subsequently reissued by both Pan books, and by Heinemann Educ. in the African Writers Series. Both reissues are in paperback.
Death and the King's Horseman (play); Methuen; London, 1977.
Myth, Literature and the African World; C.U.P.; Cambridge, 1976.

BIBLIOGRAPHIES

JAHN, Jahnheinz *A Bibliography of Neo-African Literature from Africa, America and the Caribbean*; Deutsch; London, 1965.
PARICSY, Pál *A New Bibliography of African Literature*; Academy of Science: Budapest, 1969.
RAMSARAN, John *New Approaches to African Literature: a guide to Negro-African writing and related studies*; Ibadan U.P.; Ibadan, 1965; 2nd ed. 1970.
EAST, N.B. *African Theatre: a Checklist of Critical Materials*; Africana Publ. Corp.; New York, 1970.
West Indian Literature – a select bibliography compiled by The University of the West Indies Library; Mona, Jamaica, 1964.

CRITICAL WRITINGS AND ANTHOLOGIES

ANOZIE, Sunday O. *Christopher Okigbo: Creative Rhetoric*; Africana Pubs. Union; New York, 1972.

BEIER, Ulli *African Poetry: an anthology of traditional African poems*; Cambridge U.P.; London, 1966.

BEIER, Ulli, (ed.) *Introduction to African Literature*; Longmans; London, 1967.

CARTEY, Wilfred *Whispers from a Continent. The Literature of contemporary Black Africa*; Randon House; New York, 1969; Heinemann Educ.; London, 1971.

COLLINS, Harold R. *Amos Tutuola*; Twayne; New York, 1969.

COOK, Mercer & HENDERSON, Stephen E. *The Militant Black Writer in Africa and the United States*; University of Wisconsin Press; Wisconsin, 1969.

DUERDEN, Dennis & PIETERSE, Cosmo *African Writers Talking*; Heinemann Educ.; London, 1972.

GLEASON, Judith *This Africa: Novels by West Africans In English and French*; Northwestern U.P.; Evanston, Illinois; 1965.

GOODMAN, K.L. (ed.) *National Identity*: Papers delivered at the Commonwealth Institute Conference; Queensland U.P.; Brisbane, 1968; Heinemann Educ.; London, 1970.

HEYWOOD, Christopher *Perspectives on African Literature*; Heinemann Educ.; London, 1971.

JAHN, Jahnheinz *A History of Neo-African Literature-writing in two continents*; Faber; London, 1968.

JAMES, Louis *The Islands In Between*; Oxford U.P.; London, 1968.

JONES, Eldred Durosimi *The Writing of Wole Soyinka*; Heinemann Educ.; London, 1973.

JONES, Eldred Durosimi *Wole Soyinka*; Twayne; New York, 1973.

JULY, Robert W. *The Origins of Modern African Thought, Its Development in West Africa during the 19th and 20th Centuries*; Praeger; New York, 1967; Faber; London, 1968.

KILLAM, G.D. *The Novels of Chinua Achebe*; Heinemann Educ.; London, 1969.

KILLAM, G.D. (ed.) *African Writers on African Writing*; Heinemann Educational; London , 1973

KING, Bruce *Introduction to Nigerian Literature*; Africana Publ. Corp.; New York, 1972; Heinemann Educ.; London, 1971.

KLIMA, Vladimir *Modern Nigerian Novels*; Czechoslovakian Academy of Sciences Publ. House; Prague, 1969.

LARSON, Charles R. *The Emergence of African Fiction*; Indiana U.P.; Bloomington/London, 1971; revised ed. 1972.

LAURENCE, Margaret *Long Drums and Cannons: Nigerian dramatists and novelists 1952-66*; Macmillan; London, 1968.

LO LYONG, Tabon *The Last Word: Cultural Synthesism*; East Africa Pubs. House; Nairobi, 1969.

McFARLANE, J.E. Clare *A Literature in the Making*; Pioneer Press; Jamaica, 1965.
McLEOD, A.L. *The Commonwealth Pen: An Introduction to the Literature of the Commonwealth*: Ithaca; N. York, 1961.
Mazrui, Ali *The Trial of Christopher Okigbo;* Heinemann Educ.; London, 1971.
MOORE, Gerald *Wole Soyinka*; African Pub. Corp; New York, 1971.
MOORE, Gerald *The Chosen Tongue*; Longmans; London, 1969.
MOORE, Gerald *Seven African Writers*; Three Crowns; Oxford U.P.; Oxford, 1962.
MOORE, Gerald *African Literature and the Universities*; Ibadan U.P.; Ibadan, 1965.
MOORE, G. & BEIER, U. (ed.) *Modern Poetry from Africa*; Penguin; London, 1963.
MORELL, Karen L. *In Person: Achebe, Awoonor and Soyinka*; African Studies Programme; Institute for Comparative and Foreign Area Studies; University of Washington, Seattle, 1975.
MUTISO, G.C.M. *Socio-Political Thought in African Literature: Weusi?*; Macmillan; London, 1974.
OBIECHINA, Emmanuel *An African Popular Literature: a Study of Onitsha Market Pamphlets*; Cambridge U.P.; Cambridge, 1973.
PALMER, Eustace *An Introduction to the African Novel*; Heinemann Educ.; London, 1972.
PIETERSE, Cosmo & MUNRO, Donald *Protest and Conflict in African Literature*; Heinemann Educ.; London, 1969.
PRESS, John (ed.) *Commonwealth Literature*; Heinemann Educ.; London, 1965.
RAMCHAND, Kenneth *The West Indian Novel and its Background*; Faber; London, 1970.
RAVENSCROFT, Arthur *Achebe*; British Book League; London, 1969.
REID, J. & WAKE, C. (eds.) *A Book of African Verse*; Heinemann Educ.; London, 1964.
ROSCOE, Adrian *Mother is Gold: a Study in West African Literature*; Cambridge U.P.; Cambridge, 1971.
ROSCOE, Adrian *Uhum's Fire; African Literature East to South*; C.U.P.; Cambridge, 1977.
RUTHERFORD, A. & HOLST-PETERSEN, K. (eds.) *Enigma of Values. An Introduction* (to Wilson Harris); Dangaroo Press; University of Aarhus; Aarhus, 1975.
TAIWO, Oladele *An Introduction to West African Literature*; Nelson; London, 1967.
TUCKER, Martin *Africa in Modern Literature. A survey of contemporary writing in English*; Unger; New York, 1967.

WALSH, William *Commonwealth Literature*; Oxford U.P.; Oxford, 1973.

WALSH, William *A Manifold Voice: studies in Commonwealth Literature*; Chatto and Windus; London, 1970.

WÄSTBERG, Per (ed.) *The Writer in Modern Africa*; Almquist and Wiksell; Stockholm, 1968; African Pubs. Corp.; New York, 1969.

WAUTHIER, Claude *The Literature and Thought of Modern Africa: a Survey*; Pall Mall; London, 1967.

WRIGHT, Edgar (ed.) *The Critical Evaluation of African Literature*; Heinemann Educ.; London, 1973.

ZELL, Hans & SILVER, Helene *A Reader's Guide to African Literature*; Heinemann Educ.; London, 1972. (Contains biographical, bibliographical and critical information on writers from all parts of sub-Saharan Africa.)

INDEX

Abrahams, Peter 50
Achebe, Chinua 12-23, 26-8, 31-3, 46, 49, 76, 123, 143, 144, 146, 171
Akiga, Benjamin 28
Akpan, Ntieyong Udo 28
Aluko, T.M. 28
Amadi, Elechi 28, 29, 31
Anthony, Michael 80, 84, 86-8, 91
Arden, John 163
Armah, Ayi Kwei 50-55, 62-5, 67-8, 74, 76
Arrow of God 20, 23, 27, 34
Ascent to Omai 172, 185, 188-91
Awoonor, Kofi (also Awoonor-Williams) 23, 50-52, 56, 60-62, 68-71, 74-7, 144

Beautyful Ones Are Not Yet Born, The 51, 55, 67
Beckett, Samuel 9
Beier, Ulli 60
Black Marsden 122
Brighter Sun, A 107, 122
Brother Man 120

Clarke, Austin 87
Coleridge, S.T. 181
Companions of the Day and Night 191
Concubine, The 28, 29, 31
Conrad, Joseph 9, 143, 163
Cricket in the Road 80

Dance of the Forests, A 20, 145, 146, 150, 151
Drayton, Christopher 87

Ekwensi, Cyprian, 32, 50
Eliot, T.S. 56, 57, 58, 59, 60, 143
Emigrants, The 100

Fagunwa, D.O. 140
Fanon, Franz 64, 151
Far Journey of Oudin, The 184
Fragments, 51, 53, 55, 62, 65, 67, 68

Garvey, Marcus 120
Girls at War 43
Grain of Wheat, A 36, 40
Great Ponds, The 28, 29, 30, 31

Harris, Wilson 144, 171-81, 184-6, 188-91
Hearne, John 129, 136
Heartland 184
Hills Were All Joyful Together, The 117
Hippopotamus, The 59
Hopkins, Gerald Manly 56, 60
House for Mr. Biswas, A 124, 129
Hurrah For Thunder 59

Ionesco, Eugene 9
In a Free State 123

In Person: Achebe, Awoonar, and Soyinka 151-3
In the Castle of My Skin 81, 83, 91, 94, 96, 99, 118
Interpreters, The 144, 171

James, Louis 113
Jones Eldred 144

Kongi's Harvest 149
Kill Me Quick 51

La Guma, Alex 50
Lamming, George 32-3, 80-81, 83-4, 87, 91-4, 99-100, 104, 106, 118, 135-7, 143-4, 175
Late Emancipation of Jerry Stoker, The 130
Lawrence, D.H. 143, 177
Laye, Camara 51
Limits (3) 57
Lion and the Jewel, The 20, 145
Lonely Londoners, The 104, 105

Madmen and Specialists 150, 152, 162, 163
MacKay, Claude 120
Mais, Roger 115-17, 119, 120, 134, 144
Man of the People, A 43, 47, 49, 123
Manley, N.W. 111
Mazrui, Ali 55, 56, 58, 60
MacDonald, Ian 87
Middle Passage, The 97, 99
Miguel, Street 122
Moore, Gerald 12, 28, 50, 53, 62, 112, 122
Morris, Mervyn 113
Mwangi, Meja 50, 51
My Life in the Bush of Ghosts 146
Mystic Masseur, The 122, 123

Naipaul, V.S. 83, 86, 87, 97-9, 120, 122-4, 127, 136, 143, 176
Natives of My Person 136
New Day 112, 113, 115
Ngugi, Wa Thiong'o (Also James Ngugi) 32-8, 40, 96, 143

Niven, Alistair 29, 31
No Longer at Ease 41, 42
Nwoga, Donatus I. 56, 60
Nzekwu, Onora 28

O'Casey, Sean 117
Of Age and Innocence 135, 136, 138
Okara, Gabriel 56, 144
Okigbo, Christopher 56-9, 60, 143-4
Ouloguem, Yama 51

Padmore, George 120
Palace of the Peacock 172, 177, 184, 185
Palm-Wine Drinkard, The 11
Path of Thunder: poems prophesying war 59, 60
p'Bitek, Okot 56, 62
Plains of Caroni, The 107
Post, Kenneth 22
Pound, Ezra 56, 57, 58, 143

Ramchand, Kenneth 100
Ramraj, Victor 79, 87
Ravenscroft, Arthur 43
Reid, Vic 112-13, 115-16, 129, 144
Road, The 149, 152, 153, 162, 170
River Between, The 33, 34

Salkey, Andrew 87, 129-30, 134
Sandra Street 84
Season of Anomy 171
Season of Adventure 136
Secret Ladder, The 184
Selvon, Samuel 104, 106-8, 122-3, 144
Sergeant Musgrave's Dance 163
Song of Ocol 56
Song of Lawino 56
Songs of Sorrow 56, 60, 61
Soyinka, Wole 19-20, 144-155, 161-3, 171
Suffrage of Elvira, The 122
Swift, Jonathan 162

Telephone Conversation 144
Themba, Can 50
Those Who Eat the Cascadura 107

INDEX

Things Fall Apart 12, 13, 19, 25, 26, 27, 33, 42, 146
This Earth, My Brother 68, 69, 76
Tradition and The West Indian Novel 172
Tumatumari 184
Turn Again Tiger 107
Tutuola, Amos 11-12, 140, 146

Voice, The 56

Walsh, William 22

Waiting Room, The 184
Waste Land, The 59
Water With Berries 136
Wa Thiong'o, Ngugi (See Ngugi)
Ways of Sunlight 104
Weep Not, Child 33, 35, 36
Whole Armour, The 184
Why Are We So Blest? 54, 67, 68

Year in San Fernando, The 87
Yeats, W.B. 143